WHEN GOD

GOD

SAYS NO

My Journey through Grief to Acceptance

BRENDA SMIT-JAMES

WHEN GOD SAYS NO
Copyright © 2019 by Brenda Smit-James

Some names have been changed to protect the privacy of individuals mentioned in this book.

Printed in Canada

ISBN: 978-1-4866-1763-0

Word Alive Press
119 De Baets Street Winnipeg, MB R2J 3R9
www.wordalivepress.ca

Cataloguing in Publication information can be obtained from Library and Archives Canada.

For Dad and Mom.
This is our story, as told by me.
If we could have it over again, we would change some things.
But I would never change who you were to me, my parents.

Dear Sheila,

Thank you for helping to bring this
book to life.

With deep appreciation,

Brenda

PART ONE—MOM

PART TWO—DAD

Dad and Mom, February 1997 in Johannesburg, South Africa.

ACKNOWLEDGEMENTS

This book, this account of my grief, would have remained a half-finished, abandoned, manuscript if it wasn't for the many people who contributed in bringing it to life and to completion.

It would not even have got out of my journal and onto the page if it wasn't for the encouragement, love, and support of my husband, Michiel Smit. Long before I did, he saw the joy and benefit that writing brought to my life, and the light that it brought to my eyes. Even before Mom's death, Michiel encouraged me to stop working so hard, to let go of my career, and to take time off to write. I liked the idea, a lot, but I found it difficult to let go of the financial and emotional security that my accounting work gave me. After Mom died, I remember standing in the warm winter sun in her garden and feeling the words, *it is time*, fill me. I came home to Vancouver, gave six months' notice, and stepped into my writing life.

Michiel saw potential in my writing. He saw the gift it could be to others, and also to me. He created space for my gift to flourish by keeping the home fires burning while I wrote. He kept me focused when I became discouraged in my writing and doubted its purpose. He is no doubt my most loyal critic. He is always the first editor of my work, giving me invaluable feedback and insight. My writing is stronger, better, and clearer because of his input. He has always been kind in his feedback, and at the same time, not afraid to say, "This is not your best work. You can write better than this." He has been patient with me when I have been impatient and uppity.

Time and time again he said to me, "You are a writer", and he kept saying it until I believed it. My husband is best described in the five words my brother, Grant James, said to him one sunny afternoon in June while we were having apéro drinks at a sidewalk café in Bordeaux, France. In recounting this story of how Michiel has encouraged me and created space in our lives for my writing, Grant looked across the table at Michiel and said to him, "You are a good man." Simply and succinctly said.

Michiel, my love, I am a writer and, you, you are a good man. Thank you.

I want to thank my editor, Sara Davison, for her dedicated work in editing my manuscript and for keeping my writing style on track. She has been a gift to me, giving me clear direction on both the editing, proof-reading, and publishing process. Her editing feedback has honed my skill both as a writer and as a reader. As a published writer herself, she has gone out of her way to show me the ropes and to answer my many questions. I greatly appreciate and respect her opinion and insight. I will always be grateful for her suggestion that I submit my manuscript to Word Alive Press's Women's Journey of Faith Publishing Contest.

To my brother, Mark James. Thank you for your love and support of me as your sister and as a fellow writer. Thank you for reading my manuscript, for encouraging me to tell my story, and for writing an afterword. You hold a special place in my heart.

To Andy Lambkin, pastor and friend. I am grateful for your pastoral care of me after first my mother and then my father died. You listened, and then you reached out once in a while. It was all that was needed. Over the many years we have worked together, I have come to respect your perspective. Your feedback on my manuscript, and your willingness to write the foreword, gave me confidence to continue with publishing my story.

And to those who read my manuscript as beta-readers, thank you— each of your responses helped in fine-tuning my manuscript. Sheila Rivers, your enthusiastic feedback as a reader who got caught up in the story spurred me on. John Sawyer, you highlighted the climax of the story and confirmed the weak patches I knew existed in my story writing. Mary-Louise Sawyer, your response that I have shown what it can look like to listen to and speak with God revealed a distinct theme of my writing. Julie Block, you read my manuscript not once, but twice, to help me with consistency in my writing. Thank you for your time, and for the love with which you did it. And Randy Block, thank you for asking to read my manuscript. Thank you for your heartfelt feedback and for your quiet encouragement of me as a fellow writer.

Dorian Loewen, my friend, thank you for being an emotional support and listening ear during such a difficult time in my life. Do you remember the words you spoke to me on one of our many walks during this time? In describing my emotional struggle after Mom's death, you said, "You talk about it, you don't just complain about it. You figure it out, and you do something about it. And then... you have the audacity to change." After which you added, "There's your book. You can write your book on that." Well, my friend, this is that book.

I also want to extend my thanks to those who unknowingly encouraged me at a crucial time when I lost heart and didn't think that I could finish my story. It had become too hard to visit those places of heartbreak and broken dreams. I set my manuscript aside and didn't think I would ever go back to it.

Melanie Chappell, your words encouraged me greatly, as did the pictures God gave to you of me. Your words strengthened my spirit on the long journey. Thank you for being his instrument.

Irene Robinson, whom I met for the first time at the wedding of Michiel's niece where her husband, Leigh, was the officiating pastor. Irene, the Friday night before the wedding we stood talking in the *boma* under the star-filled African sky. I got to telling you my story—it was just five months after my father's death. You encouraged me to complete my manuscript, saying that it is a story of redemption others need to hear.

Leigh Robinson, you preached a sermon on the Book of Nehemiah when we attended a service at Rosebank Union Church, Johannesburg, during that same trip to South Africa. In the sermon you asked, "What wall in your life have you been building that you have stopped building? What is the wall that you need to start building again?" I knew that it was my manuscript. I came home from that trip, opened the document on my computer, and started writing again. Thank you for your message and for your questions that Sunday. Both you and Irene were catalysts in me finishing my manuscript. Thank you.

Above all, thank you God. You have brought me a long way. It is not a journey I would have ever asked for nor would I ever want to go on it again. But this I know, regardless of what is still to come, you are faithful, and you are true. When my compass is set to you and to you alone, then I am sure of my direction and of your love to bring me through. Thank you for your great love for me.

FOREWORD

Until recently, Brenda was the accountant for the church where I serve. I say *was* because a few months ago she called to inform me that she was resigning. She said, somewhat surprisingly, that she had become a writer.

I'm glad she resigned.

Brenda was an excellent accountant. She's an even better writer. I don't mean that as it pertains to her prose. Many can write well. What makes Brenda a good writer comes from a place deeper than words. It comes from her wisdom.

What you hold in your hands is a book of wisdom. It's a memoir, to be sure. Brilliantly told, its pages will pull you along, coaxing you into reading just one more. It's a story of trial and pain, grace and joy. It's a story of how a faithful God took painful chapters and graced them with codas of redemption. But more than that, it's a story of how a little South African girl grew to become a woman of wisdom.

Lately I've been lamenting the loss of wisdom in our world. Who speaks of wisdom any longer? Lots of people talk about being smart, or creative. People everywhere boast of knowledge. But who talks about wisdom? And yet wisdom is more important by far because wisdom has to do with our relationships. It has to do with knowing what we ought to do with, and for, and because of, others.

Ought. That's the key word in all of this.

In the book of Proverbs we learn about wisdom. Solomon personifies wisdom as a lady, which seems fitting given the context. "Lady Wisdom" (as an old professor of mine named her) calls to us from the streets. She urges us toward the way we ought to live, toward what is right and prudent and just (Proverbs 1:3). In a world of whim and fancy, or selfish and vain pursuit, wisdom says to us, "but there are things we ought to do, ways we ought to live." And, as I say, this *ought* usually has to do with the people around us. Knowing what we ought to do with and for others. And, maybe most acutely, knowing what we ought to do when others and other circumstances go in a direction we had hoped they wouldn't.

That's why this is a book about wisdom. As you will read, Brenda's life has often drifted into circumstances she would not have chosen. Her life, like mine, (and yours, I presume), has been filled with people and events that have let her down. In some cases, the trials have been profound. Achingly profound. And yet, in the midst of these happenings, what bleeds through the pages are the whispers of Lady Wisdom, her instructions about how now to live, and a woman who's been learning to listen.

Brenda's memoir, as with her life, is a real treasure. Savour these pages, soak in the stories and the gift within, and may the God of all wisdom bless you as you read.

I'm confident he will.

Andy Lambkin, Pastor
North Vancouver, Canada
December 17, 2017

PROLOGUE

We are all tested in our journey of faith.

And, sometimes, our testing is so severe, so harsh, so unexpected that we find ourselves questioning our faith. We question whether what we have always believed is actually true. We question whether Jesus is worth following. We question whether we want to continue on this journey, along the narrow path.

At least I did.

My mother's death rocked my Christian beliefs, my relationship with Jesus, and my trust in God to the core. I stood emotionally traumatized, wondering where God was in all this. I questioned why I bothered to pray at all. It felt as though my prayers were ineffective before a God who had allowed circumstances to play out without intervening, which cost my mother her life.

My mother was a long-suffering, God-fearing woman, who had a deep trust in God. Her suffering and death seemed intensely unfair to me. Consequently, I encountered a side of God I had read about, but of which I'd had no personal experience. The side that is wild, untamed, and, just that, decidedly unfair, at least from our human perspective.

God stripped me emotionally bare.

He prised my mother, who meant more to me than I realized, from me and it broke my heart.

What are we to do with our broken hearts? How are we to respond when our God is silent in circumstances where his faithful suffer? How do we keep following him into the black night of the soul and not turn back? How do we find the other side of our deep grief?

Dying is difficult. And for us who are left behind, equally difficult is finding our way forward.

In her novel, *Breathing Space,* Marita van der Vyver says this, "It's terribly difficult to die ... Or to think that you are dying ... But it's just as difficult, in a way, perhaps harder ... to see someone you love slowly dying. When his [or her] pain is over, yours has hardly begun ... But it always seems to me that those left behind to go on living need more guidance than the dying."[1]

I am a writer. Hence, I was compelled to make sense of my heartache by putting it into words. For no one's benefit other than my own. But my story is not my story to keep. It is God's story. And his story is to be shared.

My prayer is that in reading my story you will identify your story in it, and that you too will see God in your story. I pray that when you do, you will find your way into his life of abundance. You will experience the truth that, even in the hard times, life is worth living. Your grief will have a purpose and you will discover what I did: he is a good God. He is love. And the circumstances and events where the wicked prosper and he appears to be absent are actually working their way towards his great plan for this world, for humanity, and for me and you.

In him, and him alone,
Brenda Smit-James
North Vancouver, Canada
October 31, 2017

PART ONE

MOM

Mom in 2011, on holiday in Brisbane, Australia.

CHAPTER ONE

Friday, June 20, 2014

I was eager to get to the hospital. I had just spent thirty-two hours commuting to Johannesburg from Vancouver. Eight of those hours had been spent sitting at Heathrow Airport watching time tick by. To cope, I had practiced patient waiting and trust in God; I had contemplated and prayed and waited. I had slept reasonably well on the flight from London to Johannesburg so I was as refreshed as I could be and now I was impatient to be with my mother. But my oldest brother wasn't in a hurry to whip me out of the airport and bear me down the highway to the General Hospital.

"Let's go get a bite to eat," Mark said. "I haven't had breakfast yet."

"I ate on the plane. I'll just have a coffee," I replied.

There really isn't an easy way to impart bad news. So Mark stated it matter-of-factly as we rode the escalator up a floor to an airport restaurant.

"Mom has leukemia."

I just nodded my head. I received the news with stillness.

We had all been hoping that Mom's news wasn't going to be too bad, that the surgeon and doctors at the hospital would save the day and that Mom would bounce back like she always did—that things were going to be just fine. But on a deeper level I knew that, this time, they weren't. When my husband saw me off at the airport in Vancouver, he wished me a good and meaningful visit with my mother. I looked at him and replied, "My mom is not going to recover from this." Later, he acknowledged that he couldn't and didn't want to believe the truth of that statement. None of us did.

The week before, a routine blood test ahead of Mom's impending surgery to remove a tumor from her face revealed what was plain for doctors to see, but that no one wanted to voice or deal with, that Mom was desperately ill. Her white blood count was dangerously low and she would not survive an operation. Her surgery scheduled for Tuesday, June 17 was cancelled and Mom was put in isolation to help her recover enough to be fit for surgery. After weeks of concern about my mother's health and what was or was not happening, as well as wondering whether her surgery was on or off, I knew I could not delay any longer. I booked my ticket for June 18, wrapped things up at work, and left for Johannesburg via Calgary and London. While I was in transit, doctors diagnosed my mother with leukemia and she was transferred from isolation in the maxi-facial ward to isolation in the cancer ward.

After breakfast, Mark wanted to stop in at a Catholic bookshop to buy a gift for one of his colleagues, a fellow priest. I let myself steep in patience. *This isn't just about me. It is also about him.* My brother had been helping to carry the load and needed a break from the hospital. And, as he advised me, the nurses didn't like us to hang around the ward. He would need to call the matron and confirm that it would be fine for him to bring me in to see Mom.

I browsed the bookshop shelves and reached for the book *Streams of Contentment* by Robert J. Wicks. I had read his book, *Riding the Dragon,* a few years before while on holiday in South Africa, had found it profound, and read it a second time, making notes of pertinent points to refer back to. I took the book with me to the counter to pay for it. Mark had finished making his purchases too, and found me at the checkout. "I called the hospital; the matron said I can bring you in to see Mom."

As we drove onto the grounds of the Jo'burg Gen, Mark pointed to the entrance. "That's where I dropped Mom on Tuesday while I went to park the car."

I glanced at the large, unwelcoming entrance and pushed thoughts of my sickly mother struggling up to its front doors without my help to the back of my mind. Mark drove to the left, away from the entrance, turned right and then right again into the parking garage. Weeds pushed up through the cement cracks and overran the garden bed. A machine dispensed a parking ticket, he retrieved it, and we drove into the blackness of the underground parking, which felt cool after the warmth of the winter sun.

From the car, Mark guided me to the escalators. "We have to walk up," he said. "The escalators don't work."

We climbed the still escalator, exiting at the top into a broad, well-lit hallway. I looked left. I looked right. I looked all around me. As a teenager in the early eighties, I remember hearing about the vastness of the Johannesburg General Hospital, of how the corridors were so wide and the hospital so big that colored arrows were painted on the ground to direct people to different departments. For a girl living in the small town of Springs on the East Rand, the hospital sounded so grand and so sophisticated, almost another world. And now, thirty years later, it looked tired, neglected, forgotten.

"Mom was in the maxi-facial ward down there first." Mark gestured to the right. "But she's now upstairs in the cancer ward. We go this way." He directed me to the left.

We approached the first set of elevators.

"We can't take these. They don't work. We need to use the ones behind them."

We found the working elevators in a dark, forbidding, unfriendly hallway where the walls were painted dark blue. We got out on the floor for the cancer ward. The windows facing the elevator reflected dullness and dirt. We turned to the right and walked down the dim hallway. At the end of the hallway, we turned right again, and pushed through double doors into the artificial brightness of the cancer ward. Mark led me around the nurses' station towards my mother's isolation room. A nurse, exiting a general ward, viewed us skeptically.

"I called earlier and got permission to bring my sister in to see my mother, Margaret James," Mark said.

The nurse pointed down the hallway to my mother's room and walked with us as we made our way to it. I heard my mother before I saw her. From down the hallway, I could make out her long, labored breaths. I barely paid attention as the nurse explained that we needed to wash our hands and wear masks in order to enter the room. We stopped. The nurse continued talking. She explained that the doctor would come and talk to us shortly. I peered through the slot of window in the door and caught the first glimpse of my mother in over a year. It was not the sight I had in mind when I said goodbye to her fifteen months before. It was a sight that was not supposed to happen: my mother ill in an isolation ward, her head turned to the right on her pillow, with a slight lift to her chin as she struggled for each of her breaths.

Oh, Mom. I felt the cry in my heart.

I tied the mask over my mouth and disinfected my hands before entering the quietness of Mom's room, punctuated every few seconds by her gasps for air. I rounded the bed, came alongside her, and reached out to touch her hand.

"Mom, I'm here."

She stirred. With enormous effort, she lifted her eyelids, just a fraction. She struggled to focus through her half-closed lids. She strained some more, until her vision appeared to clear for a moment. Her brow furrowed. Her eyes closed again. I held her hand.

"It's Brenda, Mom. I'm here."

Mark stared at me from across the bed. I stared at him. What was there to say?

CHAPTER TWO

Mom was my first best friend. Our relationship started the night I was conceived in 1966. It was the last weekend in June, winter in South Africa. The venue was the semi-detached house Mom and Dad rented at 24 Crawford Crescent, Springs. Mom had gone out for the evening with a girlfriend, leaving Dad at home to look after my two older brothers, aged three and almost fifteen months. When Mom returned home that evening, Dad was, well, in an amorous mood. As sometimes happens, one thing led to another. Afterwards, Mom was concerned about falling pregnant again. She was Catholic, she didn't use contraceptives, and she was aware of her time of the month. Dad cuddled her and said, "Don't worry about it; if you're pregnant, you're pregnant." And, being young and fertile, Mom was pregnant.

Counting out the weeks from that evening, Mom set her due date at March 26. And being a stickler for time and punctuality, I arrived on the due date, with some help from my almost two-year-old brother. As the story goes, on Saturday, March 25, 1967, my brothers were playing in the garden when the younger of my two brothers, Grant, came in to show my mother his find: a large beetle he had impaled on a fork. Mom, somewhat squeamish, was frightened by the sight and went into labor. Related events? Just perfect timing? It's anyone's guess, but that is how the story goes, and I was born in the early hours of Easter Sunday morning.

Mom had always wanted a little girl. She was close to her mother, and in turn, hoped for a daughter with whom she could be close and who would be close to her. Mom was a home-body and a mother at heart. She always wanted four children, like her mother, and included in that mix, a daughter. Her desire for a daughter was such that if it meant that she and my father would have seven sons before the daughter arrived, then so be it.

In the 1960s, husbands seldom attended the birth of their children. And so, when Mom went into labor, she was taken to the hospital and Dad packed up the two boys and headed to his parents' place to await the outcome of the birth. I was born sometime just past midnight. My grandmother received the call from the hospital, and woke my father to tell him that the latest addition to the family was a girl. "Thank God," was Dad's response. My mother had her daughter and, in his mind, the family was now complete. However, it had always been my mother's dream to have four children. My younger brother, Clinton, followed two years later.

Mom and I were close. I was her little companion. I loved being with her and going with her wherever she went, even if it was just out into the garden to hang up the washing. When I was still too small to help, I would walk between the dangling clothes and linens as if they were a maze. I particularly liked it when Mom hung sheets and towels; it made the walk even more intriguing. Still to this day, I like to hang washing. I find it comforting to peg the clothes on the line, smell the fresh laundry, and feel the warmth of the sun on my back. I like picking up the empty laundry basket and walking back inside the house. I also like to take the washing off the line, feel the crunchiness of the sun-dried towels, and the warmth of the sun on the fabric. I find it satisfying to fold the laundry and pile it up in the basket.

Mom brought me into this world, nurtured me, and loved me un-conditionally for forty-seven years until God called her home. She was an expression of God's love for me. She raised me to love the Lord.

Mom had a heart for God. She was raised Catholic and practiced her Catholic faith throughout her life. Her faith in God was her main-stay. Mom never really spoke about her beliefs; we didn't have a ritual of prayer before dinner every evening, nor was her language punctuated with references to God. But her actions were. Mom was a compassionate and kind woman. She included the excluded. She got along with most people because she was pleasing to be around. She didn't gossip, she didn't share the news of others, she kept confidences. All basic qualities that were part of the practice of her faith and rooted in the dynamics of her family.

Mom was the third daughter of deaf parents. Joseph and Eunice Hirst were both hearing at birth. Eunice, born Ranson, in Guisborough, Yorkshire, England, became deaf when she fell out of her pram as a small child and hit her head. Joseph Hirst was born in Cullinan, Pretoria, South Africa. The fifth of six children, some of Joseph's siblings were deaf. This predisposition to deafness in his family meant that a childhood illness, contracted at about the age of seven, left Joseph without his hearing. Mom and her siblings, Elizabeth, Joan, and Michael, became interpreters for their parents in a hearing world. Mom noticed how her parents were excluded from the hearing world and, as a result, she developed compassion for those who are excluded. Mom knew how to draw the outsider in; she was sensitive to the suffering of others and did not want to add to the suffering of the world.

This desire to not add to the suffering of the world was learned from her mother in the context of their Catholic faith. My grandmother had the practice of not replacing a nail if it came loose and fell out of a crucifix. Her reason was that we should not cause Jesus any more suffering. Mom carried this philosophy forward with her into her adult life. It wasn't just the nail in the crucifix, but also in her relationships with other people; Mom did not want to cause Jesus any more suffering by her actions. In Paul's letter to the Ephesians he exhorts us to "*not grieve the Holy Spirit*" (Ephesians 4:30). And in the context of relationships, he instructs us to "*be kind and compassionate to one another, forgiving each other, just as in Christ God forgave you*" (Ephesians 4:32). Mom lived this.

My mother wasn't perfect. She had her complexities and her short-comings. But it was her spirit, her faith, her unspoken motivation to live a life that was pleasing to God that directed her actions.

My mother was compassionate and kind like her Father in heaven is compassionate and kind (Luke 6:36). She smiled. She was warm and welcoming. She was liked and likeable. And I loved her.

We enjoyed each other's company. We enjoyed being together. We were friends. And yet, Mom never held onto me. It was only much later in life that I came to understand the gift of a good mother's healthy love. Mom didn't play emotional games to keep me close to her. Even when I moved away, she never hassled me with questions about when I was coming to visit or complaints that she didn't see enough of me. Mom had dreams of a relationship with her daughter in keeping with the one she'd had with her mother. One where her daughter would live close by, have at least a couple of children, and stop by for visits and a cup of tea, grandkids in tow. She would share in my adult life experiences as a mother, and we would support each other.

However, when I was in my teens, Mom noticed that I was on a different trajectory from the one she had in mind. I spoke of studies, of speaking French and moving to Paris. And children? They didn't even factor into the equation. Yet, Mom never squashed my dreams or tried to guide me in a different direction. She never manipulated me in order to make her dreams happen.

Just once, when my husband and I were in the process of immigrating to Canada, my mother spoke from a place of hurt when she mentioned that she didn't leave her mother the way I was leaving her. When I was a child, my father considered immigrating to New Zealand from South Africa, but my mother wouldn't go because she wouldn't leave her mother. And now, at the age of twenty-nine, I was leaving her to move halfway around the world. No doubt this was a great loss for my mother and she grieved the death of her dreams, and the absence of her daughter. I heard her hurt that one time and never again. Mom did not impute guilt.

Once, when I was looking in my mother's bedroom cupboard for who knows what now, I found a little girl's dress that I had made, with Mom's help, in my Grade Seven Home Economics class. It was a dress for an eight to twelve-month-old baby. It was white and sleeveless with red piping around the neck and arms. It also had splashes of bright color all over it. Mom had kept it and had it hanging in her bedroom cupboard, waiting for the day when she would give it to me for my daughter. That day never came. And I never saw the dress again. Who Mom gave it to and when she gave it away, I don't know. But when she did, it would've been with the realization that the dream she had carried in her heart was dead. Some of Mom's dreams were fulfilled, but many of her dreams died on the vine.

Now that I was middle-aged, I had dreams for Mom and me. I wanted to be more available to Mom and care for her as she aged. For my fiftieth, I wanted to surprise her with a trip to England, just the two of us. We would visit her mother's birthplace, and her half-brother Dennis, the son her mother had out of wedlock before she married my grandfather. We'd enjoy time together, like before. But now, in this hospital room, my dreams for us, like so many of her dreams had, withered and slowly died with each of Mom's labored breaths.

I took my own deep breath and looked around the room. There was nothing comforting about it, not with its stark walls, bare basics, and frosted window set high up in the wall, overlooking the isolation room next door.

The doctor came to see us and explained that they had taken further blood tests. As Mom's kidneys were failing, they planned to give her a blood transfusion to kick-start the kidneys. There was little good news. Mark and I prayed together for Mom.

"Keep going," Mark exhorted Mom after his prayer.

Keep going, when times are difficult, when troubles abound, keep going.

"You know that you are a child of God's," I said as I stroked her face.

When doubts and fears press in, hold on to the truth.

Mom tried to open her eyes again, but it was too difficult. Mark and I sensed that she had heard our prayers and that she was encouraged.

Mark left me alone with Mom for a couple of hours in the afternoon when he went to pick up Dad, who would have finished work by then. I sat by her bedside and said little. I didn't know what to say. I didn't know how to say it. I had never done this before. Perhaps if it wasn't someone I was this close to, if it wasn't my mother, I might have been able to think, I might have been able to be rational and deliberate, but instead I just sat.

When Mark returned with Dad, my father and I shared a look and embraced.

"You must be tired," Dad said, "coming straight to the hospital from the airport after two flights without much sleep and then sitting here all day."

He studied me closely and added, "But I thought you'd be sitting all day crying at your Mom's bedside. You and your mother were close."

I thought to myself, Dad, you don't know me. And yet I said nothing.

We kept vigil the rest of the afternoon. Mom appeared to slip into a light coma and seemed to be more rested and peaceful, which relieved me. Dad, Mark, and I met with the doctor in a room with three black couches and chairs pressed against the walls, all at a cold distance from each other. The room was filled with boxes. It was more a storage room than a meeting room. We asked questions, the doctor answered, he gave us information about leukemia and told us he was awaiting the results of the blood tests to determine the type. He mentioned that the treatment for leukemia was severe, but encouraged us to have hope, even though he acknowledged that it is very uncommon for one person to have three cancers in succession as Mom had, first breast cancer, then skin cancer, and now leukemia. In wrapping up our conversation, he added, "If you are having trouble with the nursing staff, let me know. I'll see what I can do, but I can't promise anything. I don't have much say here."

We spent a little more time with Mom before we headed home. I sat in the back behind Dad who was in the passenger seat. We said little as Mark negotiated the peak-hour traffic heading out of Johannesburg. The winter sun was weak. The warmth of the day was waning and the evening cold was setting in. The air would soon be filled with the coal fires of the townships. I took in the busyness of the commuters on the sidewalk. A white taxi bus, filled with customers, pulled away from the sidewalk and forced its way into the traffic. I sat. The commuters bustled.

My mother lay helpless and alone in a stark hospital room.

CHAPTER THREE

Saturday, June 21, 2014

Mark called the hospital early in the morning and spoke with the doctor after his rounds. The test results were in. Mom's leukemia was acute. The best they could do now was keep her comfortable and administer morphine. He didn't mention the 'D' word. He didn't say that Mom was dying. He didn't discuss any options with us. He didn't ask if we were able to consider palliative care for Mom. A diagnosis was made, a level of care determined. We hadn't done this before; we didn't think to ask what our options were. We were encouraged to continue to have hope and, at the same time, we were advised that we no longer needed to wear face masks.

Mark and I drove to the hospital. At the grounds entrance, a security guard stopped us. It wasn't regular visiting hours and he wanted to know why we were there. His eyes were bloodshot and he slurred his words as he questioned us. Mark told him that we were visiting our mother who was very ill. He wouldn't let us pass. Mark explained again that our mother was very ill and that we had come to be with her. Again, the guard said no, we couldn't enter.

"My mother is dying in that hospital. And I am going to go and be with her," Mark replied firmly.

The guard looked at us through bleary eyes. After a pause, he waved us through.

"What was that about?" I asked.

"He's drunk, and he wanted me to bribe him to let us in," Mark replied.

We walked into Mom's room and could immediately tell that Mom was in distress. She was in obvious pain. Any light coma that had offered relief the day before was over. If she had received morphine, it was obviously not nearly enough. Outside her room, I asked a nurse checking Mom's file if Mom had received morphine as she was in a lot of pain. The nurse looked me in the face, flipped the file towards me as if to give it to me, and said curtly, "There's no prescription for morphine here. I can't do anything without a prescription." She slammed the file down in its holder and walked away.

Stunned, I could only stand and watch her go.

I went back into Mom's room, but the sight of her distress sent me out into the hallway again.

This time, I approached the student doctor at the nurses' station.

"Excuse me. Do you know how to get hold of Dr. Jeffries?"

"Yes, why?"

"My mother is in a lot of pain and there is no prescription for morphine. He said he would leave one to keep her comfortable."

The student doctor cocked her head and frowned. "Let me check something." She moved around the desk, went down the hallway, and lifted my mother's file out of its holder. She flipped through the first few pages. Nothing. Then, from near the back of the pile of papers, tucked away, she pulled out the prescription.

"We'll get your mother's morphine."

Really? How did the prescription become buried at the bottom of a pile of papers? Surely, the doctor would have left it at the top of the file folder for the nurse to find? And if, in error, it got mixed in with some other papers, why wouldn't the nurse, knowing that the patient was in pain, not look further or make enquiries when she didn't find the prescription in the file? How could she have just walked away? If we hadn't been there to advocate for Mom, what would have happened? Would Mom have been left to struggle without morphine to relieve her pain? Would anyone have cared? And then a deeper realization struck me: what happened to those patients whose families couldn't be there to advocate for them and to see to their care when they were vulnerable, defenseless, and unable to speak for themselves?

Back in the room, I said to Mark, "Somehow, Mom's prescription got lost in the papers in her file. They're bringing her morphine."

I told him about my interaction with the nurse who said there wasn't a prescription and slammed the file down. Mark sighed.

"There are some horrible stories about this hospital," he said. "It's called the chop shop. It's the hospital of death. You don't come here to get well; you come here to die."

Mark stroked Mom's hand. "Earlier this week, I was in the lift and two doctors were talking openly about how they couldn't wait to get out of this hell hole and into private practice. The funds that are supposed to come to the hospital are not all getting here, the money is being spent elsewhere."

I didn't have to think too hard about where those funds might be spent. News reports were full of President Jacob Zuma and the ruling ANC elite living the high life out of the government coffers. The scandal related to President Zuma spending R246 million of state funds on his private residence was still full blown. Money the government had previously spent on health care and infrastructure was no longer getting to where it needed to be. And this was surely evident at the Jo'burg Gen. A small group of elite people were becoming fabulously wealthy. The poor, and those who couldn't afford the cost of private medical care, were paying for it with their lives.

When another nurse finally arrived to administer the morphine, we exchanged no words or pleasantries. She was as disinterested in us as she was in her patient. An hour later the morphine had not taken effect. Mom was still in distress. And I too was in distress.

I found another student doctor at the nurses' station.

"My mom is still in a lot of pain. Is it possible to give her more morphine?" I asked.

She snorted. "We don't want to kill her."

"I don't want to kill her either; I just want to help her."

The student doctor looked at me with disdain. I walked away.

That afternoon close family visited. We could all see Mom's pain and suffering.

"Why don't they give her oxygen?" my cousin, Shirley, asked.

"I don't know. Will it help?"

"Well, your Mom won't struggle so much to breathe. Yes, it will help."

What should I do? I felt that there was nothing to be done. When my uncle, Brian, and cousin, Devin, visited, Devin mentioned that he had connections with a few doctors who might help us know how to access oxygen on a weekend. He would see what he could do.

Early in the evening we left. It was hard to leave Mom like that, but we couldn't stay. The nurses preferred that we go.

"I understand the verse in the Bible that says that the wages of sin is death better now," I said to Mark as we walked to the elevator. "I always understood it to mean that because of sin we will die, but this shows me that the dying process is also the penalty for sin. It's hard."

That night I went to bed early. It had been a hard day so I left Mark to update my youngest brother Clinton and his wife Tracy, with whom we were staying. Unfortunately, after three hours of sleep, I found myself wide awake. I looked at the clock; it was only 11 pm. Restless, I sat up in bed and switched on the lamp. My thoughts were with Mom, struggling in the room on her own. *How is she doing now? Does she feel as though we have abandoned her?* I was anguished by Mom's suffering and by my powerlessness to effect change or even relief for her. Thoughts whirled through my head. In my distress, I needed to know that the Lord knew what it was to suffer. I couldn't serve a God who did not know suffering himself, who could not identify with what we were experiencing.

I opened my Bible to the Gospel of Matthew and read about Jesus' suffering in the Garden of Gethsemane. I read how Jesus "*began to be sorrowful and troubled*" (Matthew 26:37) and that he said to the apostles, Peter and the two sons of Zebedee, "*My soul is overwhelmed with sorrow to the point of death. Stay here and keep watch with me*" (Matthew 26:38).

Even the Son of God wanted company in his distress. He didn't want to be alone. Jesus asked his disciples to keep watch with him and to pray.

The disciples could not remove his suffering, but they could partake in it through prayer and by keeping him company. I felt a stirring within. We needed to go back to keep Mom company during the long night and to pray for her.

A sound caught my attention. Mark stood outside my door speaking to someone. He had also gone to bed early, but clearly was having as much trouble sleeping as I was. I opened the bedroom door to find him right outside talking with Tracy.

His eyes met mine. "I think we need to go back."

I nodded.

Mark didn't want to drive into Johannesburg in the dead of night on our own. It didn't feel safe. He called one of his colleagues, Brian, the parish priest at Springs Catholic Church, to ask him to drive us back to the hospital.

Once we were there, the nurses opened the security gate to the cancer ward and let us in to see Mom. She was still in pain, her breathing strained.

"I was here just after seven this evening." Brian joined us at the side of the bed. "Your mom was in a lot of pain then too."

"We can't leave her alone like this," I replied. "I think we should stay the night."

Mark nodded. "I'll go and speak with the nurses."

Brian and I remained in the room. We didn't talk. I caressed Mom's hand.

Mark returned from the nurses' station. "We can stay the night, but only one of us can be in the room at a time."

"Then we can take turns with one of us in the room and the other waiting in the hallway," I determined.

"No, the nurses only want one person on the premises," Mark clarified. "Besides which, it's better that one of us is rested and can take over in the morning."

I decided to stay. Soon after Mark went home with Brian, I stuck my head into the hallway. A nurse was looking at Mom's file.

"Excuse me." I smiled. "Do you know when my mother had morphine last?"

"Around 10 or 11," she responded, and moved away.

I dimmed the lights in Mom's room, took her hand, and prayed out loud for her above the coarseness of her breathing. But her distress caused me distress, and my prayer reflected that; my words were rushed, my voice high-pitched, my tone pleading, and any source of comfort ineffective.

I texted my husband on the Blackberry I had with me. It was Saturday afternoon in Vancouver and the early hours of Sunday morning in Johannesburg. In my anguish, I poured out my heartache to him. He was shopping at a large grocery store, filling the cart with food and trying to text-comfort his wife at the same time.

I'm almost done, he wrote, let me get home and I will text you.

Within thirty minutes we were communicating again. Michiel suggested that I read a passage from Isaiah that he had been meditating on and praying through for us.

"To whom will you compare me? Or who is my equal?" says the Holy One.
Lift up your eyes and look to the heavens:
Who created all these?
He who brings out the starry host one by one and calls forth each of them by name.
Because of his great power and mighty strength, not one of them is missing.
Why do you complain, Jacob?
Why do you say, Israel,
"My way is hidden from the LORD;
My cause is disregarded by my God?"
Do you not know? Have you not heard?
The Lord is the everlasting God, the Creator of the ends of the earth.
He will not grow tired or weary,
And his understanding no one can fathom.
He gives strength to the weary and increases the power of the weak.
Even youths grow tired and weary, and young men stumble and fall;
But those who hope in the Lord will renew their strength.

They will soar on wings like eagles; they will run and not grow weary,
They will walk and not be faint. (Isaiah 40:25-31)

I read it silently, then out loud to Mom, praying it over her. I sat. My spirit was quiet. Mom too was noticeably less agitated. Our spirits were quiet together.

I awoke a little later, after having fallen asleep to Mom's rhythmic breathing. The Word of God had comforted us and we had both slept. Yet, Mom was starting to labor again with her breathing. Her distress was increasing. I looked at the time. It was 4:30 in the morning. A nurse had not come in to check on Mom in the time that I had been there. If she had, she would have needed to turn on the lights to see well. It had certainly been more than four hours since Mom's last morphine injection. In fact, based on the nurses' earlier information, it could have been five hours, if not six, since the last dose was administered.

I couldn't wait any longer. I went to the nurses' station and approached the nurse who had been outside the room earlier.

"Excuse me, please."

She looked up from her computer monitor.

"Is it possible for my mother to receive her next dose of morphine?"

"Yes, we'll bring it," she replied.

The same nurse arrived to administer the morphine. I was relieved because she had a slightly friendlier demeanor.

"Do you like nursing?" I asked her.

"Yes," came the reply.

"What do you like about it?" I asked, eager to engage her somewhat.

She looked at me quizzically, administered the dose, and before she left replied, "It's what I have always wanted to do."

Thankfully, this time, after the injection, Mom was more settled.

Later, two nurses came in to bathe Mom. I left the room to give them space, but stood outside the closed door and watched through the window. The nurses unceremoniously tipped Mom onto her side to wash her back. Her eyes flew open, wild with pain. I was shocked. The nurses were oblivious as they performed their duty. My heart broke and I looked away. *Oh Mom*, I cried in the depths of my being, *I am so sorry.*

After the nurses left, I entered the room. Mom's eyes were closed again; she could not lift her eyelids. I touched her hand and said nothing. If I tried to speak, I would lose it, and I needed to stay composed. I pushed the picture of her eyes flying open wide with pain aside.

Time passed slowly as I waited for Mark to come and relieve me. I walked around the windowless room and stopped to read a notice next to the door. It was a check list for everything that was operational in the room. It had last been checked a few days before. Listed was an outlet for oxygen and oxygen equipment. My eyes widened. Oxygen was available? Why hadn't it been offered or administered to help relieve Mom's pain or to assist with her breathing? Just the bare minimum, if that, was all that was being done. I scanned the room. Above the bedside table on the left was an outlet. I scrutinized it. It was an oxygen outlet, clearly labeled. The equipment was stored directly below it, tucked behind the bedside table. Comfort was inches from her head, but not being offered. My shoulders slumped, and a sigh lodged deep within me. *Oh Mom.*

Mark arrived at 6:00 am with Dad, who had come to see Mom and to take me home.

We talked outside the room so Dad could have time alone with Mom.

"All that time we spent yesterday talking with Devin about trying to arrange to bring oxygen in for Mom was a waste of time," I told him. "There's oxygen in the room. It's right there behind the bedside table."

Mark looked at me with disbelief and exhaled loudly.

"I don't know why we have to ask for everything," I continued. "It's all there, and in working order. Assuming that the check list behind the door is to be believed."

"It probably has to do with cost," Mark explained. "There isn't a lot of money available so they are saving it wherever they can."

"So Mom has to suffer and go without!" I glanced though the window at Mom. Dad, quiet beside her bed, was looking at her and shaking his head.

"When Dr. Jeffries comes to see Mom on his rounds at 8 o'clock, please ask him to let Mom have oxygen," I instructed Mark. "In fact, insist on it. I realize that cost may be an issue, but right now our concern is Mom, nothing else."

Mark nodded.

"And the morphine, ask him to increase the dosage, or at least give Mom a sedative. We can't let her suffer like this any longer."

"I will." Mark reached out and touched my arm. "I've had enough of this too."

Mark told me later that, once he was alone with Mom, he witnessed the first of Mom's death throes. After lying unmoving for days, her head placid on the pillow, Mom's head lurched suddenly to the left, her eyelids opened and her eyes rolled back in their sockets. She stopped breathing and life drained out of her face. She went gray. A few seconds later, she took another breath and color flooded back into her cheeks. The episode was violent and he was shocked.

"I didn't know what to do, so I went to tell the student doctor on duty. The one who is pregnant," he recounted to me.

"I am sorry it is so difficult to watch," she had said, "but apparently the dying don't feel this."

"Well, we won't know that for sure until it is our turn to be lying in the bed, will we?" Mark had replied.

I held my tongue and said nothing when Mark told me the story.

Yet, I wondered, *how would she like it if it was her child, or her mother, lying in the bed one day?*

When the oncologist visited Mom during his rounds that morning, he agreed to give Mom oxygen and he administered medication to take the edge off the death throes.

CHAPTER
FOUR

Johannesburg General Hospital had been renamed Charlotte Maxeke Johannesburg Academic Hospital on September 29, 2008, but it was still often referred to under the abbreviation of its original name, Jo'burg Gen.

Charlotte Maxeke (née Mannya) was born in 1874 in the Polokwane district of South Africa and moved to the Eastern Cape at a young age. She and her family later moved to Kimberley where she trained as a school teacher. When she obtained her B.Sc. degree from Wilberforce University, Ohio, USA, she became one of the first black South African women graduates. In university, she met her future husband, fellow South African Marshall Maxeke. After completing their studies, they returned to South Africa in 1901.

It was while attending Wilberforce University that Charlotte Maxeke, already a dedicated churchgoer, was influenced by the African Methodist Episcopal Church with which the University was affiliated. On returning to South Africa, she established the African Methodist Episcopal Church and was the organizer of the Women's Mite Missionary Society in Johannesburg. She and her husband established a school in Evaton, south of Johannesburg, and they went on to teach and evangelize in other areas of South Africa, including the Transkei.

On a trip to London in 1891 as a member of the African Jubilee Choir, Charlotte Maxeke performed for Queen Victoria. While in

London, she was influenced by the suffragette movement and suffragette speakers such as Emmeline Pankhurst. Later, Charlotte Maxeke would advocate for black South African women, both politically and socially. This included fighting for freedom from exploitative social conditions for African women. Politically, Charlotte Maxeke attended the launch of the South African Native National Congress in Bloemfontein in 1912 and she participated in the formation of the Industrial Commercial and Worker's Union in 1920.

In her political and social endeavors, Charlotte Maxeke moved in multiracial arenas. She spoke at the Women's Reform Club in Pretoria, which was concerned with the voting rights of women, and she was a member of the Joint Council of Europeans and Africans, initiated in Johannesburg in 1921 to facilitate discussion and practical co-operation between races, so as to improve the social and economic conditions of Blacks, Coloreds, and Indians in South Africa.

Charlotte Maxeke died in Johannesburg in 1939, and sixty-nine years later the Johannesburg General Hospital was renamed the Charlotte Maxeke Johannesburg Academic Hospital in her honor.

The hospital is, as its name suggests, a teaching hospital. Such an auspicious name easily inspires confidence and images of medical education and efficiency, with doctors and nurses receiving top-notch training and the opportunity to develop and hone their skills. However, our experience over those four days, as well as the numerous accounts I heard of Mom's experience, paint a different picture. The hospital's patients are the poor, and those who cannot afford the prohibitive cost of private medical insurance in South Africa. My mother fell into that second category. Financial constraints, and a belief shared with my father that parents should not live off their children, meant that Mom and Dad could not afford private medical insurance. And so, when Mom got sick, first with breast cancer and then with skin cancer, she relied on the public health care system at Jo'burg Gen to care for her.

Mom was diagnosed with breast cancer in August 2009 and her initial experience with the hospital was a good one. Her chemotherapy treatment through the cancer department at Jo'burg Gen was caring and effective. When she was operated on as a day-patient for skin cancer on her top lip in August 2012, the operation by the trainee plastic surgeon was successful. The scar that ran from just below Mom's nose and into her top lip was barely discernible. Based on her experience thus far, Mom trusted the public medical system at the hospital. However, her third experience was not a good one.

In December 2013, Mom consulted a private maxi-facial surgeon with regard to a swelling in her mouth. He determined that it was an abscess. Mom and Dad paid R20,000 cash for the surgeon to cover the cost of lancing the abscess in his consulting room. He fit Mom in quickly before his Christmas holidays, pulling two teeth and draining the swelling. In January, Mom returned to ask about the lump that was still prominent.

"Don't worry, it will go away," he replied. It didn't.

In February 2014, Mom decided to see the plastic surgeon at Jo'burg Gen who had overseen the operation for skin cancer on her lip by the trainee plastic surgeon. At her consultation, he said that there was nothing that he could do for her and transferred her to the Maxi-Facial department. Consultations were held on a Monday and consultations that were not completed on the day were held over until the following week. If the Monday was a public holiday, there were no consultations until the following week.

Over the next couple of months, the Maxi-Facial department took their time assisting Mom. On Mondays, Tracy would drive Mom to Jo'burg Gen at the crack of dawn so that she could be one of the first in the line at the hospital. Some Mondays Mom would return home disappointed that there had been no progress, even after being at the hospital all day. Or, other Mondays, she was sent for X-rays, would wait for hours to be X-rayed, and return to the Maxi-Facial department only to find that there was no one to help her. She had to take her X-rays home with her and wait until the following Monday to hand them over. Mom was admitted to hospital for some tests, but after two days of being in hospital with little being done, she left.

Time was wasted, the care was poor, the diagnosis was slow in coming, the treatment was non-existent, and the so-called abscess grew.

At her Monday consultation at the beginning of May, after two successive Mondays of public holidays and, subsequently, no consultations, Mom was advised by the junior administrative person at the front desk that there was nothing the Maxi-Facial department could do to assist her and she was referred to the Ear-Nose-Throat department. Mom was frustrated and furious.

"You have wasted two months of my life!" she yelled.

She went home broken, but called the ENT department and got an appointment for two Mondays later, May 19.

I knew some of this from what Mom recounted to me when I called her. What I didn't know was just how serious the issue was. Mom constantly referred to it as an abscess, so that is what I thought it was. When we conversed, she spoke in a relatively upbeat tone. Hence I was reassured. In her emails, she always encouraged me not to worry. So I didn't. Mostly. And no one told me otherwise.

Sunday, May 11, 2014 was Mother's Day. Michiel and I called to wish Mom a Happy Mother's Day. Her guard was down and she couldn't pretend anymore. She couldn't keep it together and protect me any longer. She was depressed and crying. She spoke about the awful abscess on her face and how it had burst and how she felt so unclean.

"And it stinks. It weeps continually," she said.

She hated how it looked on her face.

"Mom," I asked, "how does an abscess break through your skin? I thought an abscess was in your mouth."

"It's awful. I have this huge sore on my face. It is so ugly."

Mom talked. We listened. My heart broke for her.

"Do you want me to send you a photo so you know what it looks like?" she asked.

Why hadn't we thought of that before?

"Yes," I replied. "Because I can't picture it."

"Okay," Mom said. "I'll ask Tracy to take it for me and I'll send it you."

Mom was a little more cheerful when we hung up, but my heart was heavy.

The next night when I get home from work, Michiel said, "Your Mom emailed the photo."

I sat down at the desk and opened the email, then the attachment. On the screen I saw the side profile of my mother's face. No words would come; I just sat and shook my head. *This is serious.*

That night I forwarded the picture in an email to Mark, and copied my brother Grant who lived in Australia to express my concern and ask what was going on. Mark replied that he too was concerned. He had long believed that the situation was more serious than anyone wanted to acknowledge. In his opinion, none of the doctors wanted to deal with the issue and so were stalling and passing Mom along to different departments. Afterwards, I called Mom but there wasn't anything she could do until her appointment with the Ear, Nose, and Throat Department the following Monday.

The ENT doctor who met with Mom on Monday, May 19, was kind and helpful. She reviewed Mom's file and said that she would need to consult with her colleagues as to a course of action and Mom should come back that Thursday. If she wasn't in the consulting room, she encouraged Mom to look for her on the ward, and she would advise as to the treatment to consider.

Mom went back on the Thursday and found the doctor on the ward. Unfortunately, she had forgotten about Mom and had not discussed her file at the meeting with her colleagues. She apologized and told Mom to come back again the following week.

This doctor did try to be proactive and help Mom. After consultation with her colleagues, it was determined that Mom would need major surgery to remove the tumor and reconstruct her jaw bone. At one of her subsequent visits to the hospital, the ENT doctor requested that the plastic surgeon Mom had consulted in February come look at Mom's face.

My mother's cousin, Colin, was with Mom at that appointment to offer her his moral support. He told me how the plastic surgeon arrived, ripped the gauze and padding off Mom's face without any care or consideration for the pain it caused her, looked at the tumor, said nothing, and walked away. When Mom and Colin left the hospital that day, Mom could not take the strain of the treatment anymore. At the elevator she leant against Colin, broke down, and sobbed.

Stories unfolded of patients being shouted at by doctors and nursing staff alike. For most patients, Jo'burg Gen was the sole place they had any hope for treatment. Their only other option was to go home and let their illness take its course and die a slow death. Mom exercised the choices that she had.

After the poor treatment from the private maxi-facial surgeon in Benoni in December, and during the slow treatment at the Jo'burg Gen, Mom paid for private treatment to have the tumor swabbed and tested for cancer. The private doctor's response was that it wasn't cancerous. There was a small bit of a squamous cell carcinoma present, but he wasn't worried about it. The day Mom received that news, she drove home elated. She called my father on his cell phone at work and could not speak because she was crying so much from the relief. Dad left work immediately after letting his employer know that he had to go and care for Mom. He consoled her and had a cup of tea with her before going back to work.

Mom had her own experience of doctors shouting at her. In May, when Mom was depressed and suffering from an acute bladder infection, Mark visited her. He was living a five-hour drive away at the time and so was not often available to help. He took one look at Mom and realized that she was not well at all. He called a doctor friend of his and rushed Mom through to Jo'burg to see him. Mark's friend gave Mom medication for her bladder infection, checked her tumor, and said he didn't think it was cancerous. He heard Mom's story about the treatment—or lack thereof—at the hospital. He decided to write a letter to the doctors to raise the issue of their poor treatment of her. When Mom went back to the hospital for a check-up, the doctors lambasted Mom for seeking outside medical treatment, and for reporting to another doctor that their treatment of her was poor.

I heard too of how Mom would come to the hospital for treatment and her heart would go out to the poor who walked the halls of the hospital begging for taxi fare so they could get home after their chemotherapy treatment. Or they begged so that they could buy food and some supplies to soften their stay in hospital. Their families were too poor to afford the taxi fare to come to the hospital to assist them. Mom helped wherever she could.

The sterility and cleanliness of the hospital was also a concern. While attending to Mom, I mentioned to Mark how I flicked a cockroach off Mom's bed.

"This cancer ward is one of the better ones in the hospital," he said. "You should have seen the maxi-facial ward where Mom was first. It was terrible."

I had to wonder if Charlotte Maxeke would be honored or embarrassed to have her name attached to this hospital if she were alive to see it today.

CHAPTER FIVE

Monday, June 23, 2014

I awoke at 4 am and went next door into Mark's darkened room.

"Mark, are you awake?"

"Yeah," he replied, groggily.

"I think we should go and relieve Grant. He's been there all night and he'll be tired from his flight."

Grant, my older brother, had arrived from Australia late on Sunday afternoon. After freshening up with a shower, he had gone with Mark to see Mom. That evening Mark returned alone; Grant had decided to stay with Mom and sit with her through the night.

"You're right." Mark yawned and sat up in bed. "But let me check with Clinton. Perhaps he wants to drive in and get Grant."

It was helpful that, at this difficult time, my youngest brother and his wife had a house big enough to accommodate me, my two older brothers, and their two teenage sons, Jared and Dylan. And since Dad and Mom lived in a small cottage on the property, Dad was close by too.

Mark returned from speaking with Clinton.

"Tracy has already gone to pick Grant up."

An hour earlier, Tracy, unable to sleep, had apparently gone outside onto the verandah and lit a cigarette. Alone in the quiet of the dark cold morning, smoking her cigarette, she had heard my mother's voice speak to her as clearly as if Mom was standing next to her. *Tracy, come and get Grant. He's tired.*

Startled, Tracy replied out loud, "I'm coming." She'd stubbed out her cigarette, woken up Clinton to let him know she was heading out, and driven alone into Johannesburg to pick up Grant.

Knowing that Grant would be home soon, and after agreeing that Mark would take the morning shift, we both headed back to bed.

Later, I arrived at the hospital around noon with Mom's cousin, Colin, and his wife Belinda to relieve Mark. Through the glass panel in the door, I saw that Mark wore a face mask again. He indicated that we needed to put them on too before he came and met us at the door. Mom had rallied; her heart was much stronger and the oncologist had advised that we needed to resume wearing the face masks. According to Mark's report from the doctor, Mom's vital signs had improved greatly. Her chest had cleared somewhat and her blood pressure was better, but her kidneys were failing again. She was lucid and had been very emotional when her brother, Mike, and her sister-in-law and long-time friend Doreen had said their goodbyes. Mark appeared upset, and left shortly after we arrived.

As soon as we entered the room, I greeted Mom. She was facing away from the door, so Colin and Belinda walked over to the other side of the bed. When Mom saw them, a tear slipped out of her left eye; her tear ducts were working again. She tried to speak to Colin from behind the oxygen mask, but only a grunt came out of her dry mouth. Her eyes were filled with pain and an emotion I couldn't quite discern—fear, concern, urgency? Colin and Belinda came around to the other side of the bed, where I stood, so they were out of Mom's line of sight.

"We're going to leave because it's upsetting your mom," Colin said.

They returned to the other side of the bed and said their goodbyes. I saw them to the door, shut it behind them, and returned to comfort Mom.

"It's okay, Mom. Shhh..." I stroked her cheek tenderly and kissed her dry forehead. Her restless spirit settled again in her inert body. Her breathing rasped.

With Mom settled, I went into the adjoining bathroom to talk with God. On Saturday afternoon, Mark had administered the Last Rites, the Catholic sacraments for the dying, and we had prayed for and over

Mom. On one level, we had prepared her and ourselves for her death, which made the change in Mom's vital signs, and this extension of hope, confusing.

I asked either for a full, miraculous healing for Mom or no healing at all. I asked that God take her home rather than allow her to continue to suffer. Summoning the strength to fight the long road of leukemia was no life for her. I did know, though, that her improvement was likely temporary. It's not uncommon for the dying to rally just before the end. It is an opportunity to say goodbye. So any hope extended to us by the doctor was likely misplaced.

In the afternoon, a nurse I hadn't seen before entered the room to take Mom's blood pressure. I greeted her.

"Hello, I'm Brenda. This is my mother. Her name is Margaret."

Perhaps, just perhaps, she would see my mother as a person and treat her with dignity. Unfortunately, she responded with a patronizing, "Hello, Margaret."

I wanted to smack her, yet I had learned very quickly that power was not in my hands. Mark and I had discussed that we needed to stay on the right side of the nurses as we didn't know what they would do to Mom when we weren't there. Their lack of care and compassion when we were there was hard enough to witness.

The nurse took Mom's blood pressure, ripping apart the Velcro when she finished. Mom's arm flopped out at the pull and she winced. I reached across and tried to catch her arm. The nurse noticed. Maybe, just maybe, she would realize that it hurt and treat the next patient with more consideration. Care for the sick, dignity for the dying, were sorely lacking for my mother.

Karen, the daughter of Mom's friend of over forty years, also named Margaret, brought her mother to visit with Mom. Karen was a nurse and volunteered at the Jo'burg Gen in the maternity ward. She had stopped in that morning to see Mom and, realizing that Mom did not have long, she called her own mother to say that if she wanted to see Margaret she must come right away, not later in the week as planned.

Karen and I left the room to give our mothers time together. She reviewed Mom's file, and for the first time in four days I got a clear picture of my mother's condition without any false hope blended in. She showed me the sheet with that day's entry, June 23. The instruction was palliative care, yet we had not been told that. So why had the doctor insisted that we wear masks again? Why did he speak in vague terms and encourage Mark not to give up hope? Hope for what? A miracle?

I know miracles happen; I have seen them with my own eyes. But I wish that the doctor had explained the whole picture to us, the real picture. I wish that he had told us he was administering palliative care and why. I wish that he had told us that it is not uncommon for the dying to rally on their last day and that this was the time for goodbyes. I wish that he had told us that it was just a matter of time. I wish, instead of offering weak platitudes, he had asked us if we were people of faith and encouraged us to pray, knowing that life and death are in God's hands. I wish he hadn't filled us with half-truths and false hope. What if we hadn't known that, in spite of her improvements, she would not likely live much longer? What if we had not taken this opportunity to be with her and to say our farewells?

Talking with Karen, it was so good to be treated as an adult at last. It was good to get clarity and to no longer be sent in circles, confused, not sure what the actual situation was or what we should do. Karen showed me the other entries in the report. The doctor had noted that Mom's breast cancer was in remission and that she had acute leukemia as a result of chemotherapy for the treatment of breast cancer. He also noted that the squamous cell carcinoma on her face had metastasized. Why had we not been told any of this?

I shared my experiences with the nursing staff—their lack of compassion and their poor care—with Karen.

"Unfortunately," Karen said, "the staff is not trained in palliative care. Your mom should be turned every four hours."

I blinked. Every four hours? Mom hadn't been turned in four days except to be unceremoniously tipped on her side for a bed bath. And that had caused pain for her and trauma for me.

Sitting alone again at Mom's bedside, I touched her hand, now clasped into a fist. I uncurled her fingers and gasped at the sight of the awful bedsore on the ring finger of her left hand. If her finger looked like this from just one day, what did her back look like after four days? My heart broke further. *Oh Mom, we are doing this so poorly. You don't deserve this.* I placed her opened hand on the sheet next to her, but in a short while her fingers curled in again.

I started to talk to her. It was natural for me to say my goodbyes. I told her how much I loved her. I told her that I had revealed to Michiel that, second to him, I loved my mother the most of anyone in the world.

"No, you love your mother more than you love me," he had replied.

I had to acknowledge that he was right. I shared that with my mother too.

I told her the things we need to tell our loved ones. I told her to go on, and that I would join her one day in heaven, where we would be together. I told her not to worry about Dad and her grandsons, we would take care of them. Her time was done. She was free to go. When Clinton and Tracy came to pick me up, I offered my last words to my mother. I kissed her dry, salty forehead and said, "Bye, Mom. I know I will see you again."

I left the room and waited outside so my brother and his wife could spend some time saying their goodbyes. I needed a breather. I was overwhelmed. My senses were overloaded. While I waited, Grant arrived to do the night vigil. He had stopped to do some shopping for Mom. He wanted to wash her, as best he could, care for her, show her love and treat her with dignity, and he had bought what he needed. Clinton and he moved Mom to reposition her. She responded in pain, the drip pulled out of her hand, and she bled on to the sheet.

That night, at the dinner table, we started to talk about options for palliative care. Now that we knew for sure that it was only a matter of time, our thoughts extended to how we could best take care of her. Things could not continue as they were. We could no longer leave her in the care of the hospital. We started to make enquiries as to our options.

At 8:30 pm, Mark's cell phone rang. It was Grant, calling to let us know that Mom had passed away about fifteen minutes before, and that the doctor had just confirmed her death. I started to cry. My nephew, Jared, came around the table and put his arm around me. We were all quiet. A dog barked.

Tracy went across to the cottage and knocked on the bedroom window to wake Dad. My younger nephew Dylan and I joined my father and sister-in-law in the cottage. Dad looked shocked as he embraced Tracy, consoling her. He consoled me too as I cried.

Mark and Clinton decided to go to the hospital to assist Grant. I wanted to go back with them to see Mom one last time, but instead I chose to stay behind with Dad.

Dylan and I rejoined my father in the cottage and I put on the kettle for tea. Dad sat in his usual spot at the kitchen counter, his back against the wall. As I waited for the water to boil, we caught each other's eyes. He had been crying, but I chose to say nothing. I finished making the tea and passed him his cup.

When my brothers returned from the hospital, Mark told us how Grant had covered Mom with a beautiful red blanket and that she looked like royalty, a queen, lying in the bed. How fitting it was that, when she left this earth to be taken into heaven, she was covered with dignity and a display of love by her son.

Grant recounted how, when Mom stopped breathing, he went to call the doctor on duty. He had no sooner said, "Excuse me," when she replied, "Now what?"

"I think my mother has died," Grant replied. "Can you please come and check?"

She did come to check. She looked in Mom's eyes and she blew with an instrument into her ear. She turned to Grant, with tears in her eyes, and said, "Yes, your mother has died."

That evening, inspired by words from Job 14, I wrote in my journal:

Life born of woman is of few days and full of trouble. She springs up like a flower and withers away; like a fleeting shadow she does not endure. Our days are determined; you, O God, have decreed the number of our months and have set limits we cannot exceed. Mom dies and is laid low; she breathes her last and is no more. She lies down and does not rise. If a woman dies, will she live again?

CHAPTER SIX

I awoke with a start, my eyes flying open. After the vivid dream I'd just had, I expected to see a horse looming over me, face-to-face, its eyes blazing into mine and steam emanating from its nostrils. Instead, my gaze took in the oval-mirrored antique wardrobe against the wall next to my bed and the thatched roof above my head.

"Lord, what was that about? What am I supposed to do with the horse?" I lay still, staring at the wardrobe. "Am I supposed to get on it? What are you saying to me?"

The questions stirred deep in my soul.

The reply came. "Brenda, how you respond to your mother's death will determine how much more of my strength and power I will give you."

The words were a challenge, a gauntlet thrown to the ground.

Like the horse, the dream had been swift and powerful. I was in a field and a dark horse, full of vigor, came from the right to pass in front of me. He epitomized power as he ran; his muscles rippled under his glistening coat. He was vibrant, vital with life and strength. I watched, confident from my vantage point that he would continue on his course across the field. Yet, he turned sharply and ran right at me, stopping immediately in front of me. His large blazing face looked straight down into mine. Fear overwhelmed me and I awoke.

This was a God-given dream. The questions that stirred in my soul confirmed that. The Lord's response sealed it.

Michiel stirred. I hunkered under the covers and tucked myself in next to him. The room was cold. After Mom's funeral I had wanted to get away for a while. I couldn't bear to be in Johannesburg any longer. I needed to go somewhere I could breathe. Unfortunately, it was the winter school holiday and many places were already booked. But Michiel found accommodation for us at Wyndford Holiday Farm, outside Fouriesburg on the Lesotho border. Nineteen years earlier, Michiel had proposed to me at the Farm when we had attended a directors' meeting there for Wycliffe Bible Translators South Africa, but we had not been back for nearly as many years. We rented a small thatched cottage and took our meals in the Farm's dining room. Winter nights in the Free State are cold. The cottage had only a small, barely-adequate heater to warm the room. I wriggled farther under the covers.

"Are you okay?" Michiel nudged closer to me.

"I had a disturbing dream." I proceeded to describe it to him.

"Do you want to have a cup of tea and get up?"

"Yes, please."

Michiel got out of bed. He filled the kettle with water and switched it on. While he busied himself with making tea, I reached for my Bible and the devotional *Jesus Calling* by Sarah Young. I turned to the reading for that day, July 8. As I read, a stillness came over me; God's guidance to me through it was direct and clear.

The reading spoke of seeking Jesus' face alone, and of opening our hearts and our minds "to receive more and more" of Jesus so as to know what it is to taste eternal life in the "here and now."[2] The day's reading ended with, *"For now we see only a reflection as in a mirror; then we shall see face to face"* (1 Corinthians 13:1).

I underlined the words "receive more and more of Me" and also *"we shall see face to face."* The horse was my face-to-face encounter with Jesus. I sensed that it was up to me to decide how I would process the hard journey of deep grief. Would I look to Jesus face to face, and grapple with my questions and my loss? Or would I turn away? And should no answers to my questions be forthcoming, would I respond with acceptance and submission, or rejection and rebellion? The challenge was before me: Was I going to rise to the occasion? Would I tap into my fighting spirit? How deep was I willing to go?

This was not the first time on the journey with Mom that God had challenged me and warned me.

Towards the end of April, I started to get a sense that her lack of treatment and care from the hospital over the last few months was wearing her down and that her condition very much needed attention. As I prayed for healing for my mother, a regular response from God was, "Brenda, pray so that you do not fall into temptation." Those were the same words Jesus said to Peter ahead of Peter's testing at the time of Jesus' arrest and subsequent crucifixion.

I would cry out and the reply would come, "My way is above your way; my thoughts above your thoughts."

I would fall on my knees for my mother, asking and pleading. And God would say, "Get up and pray that you will not fall into temptation. Pray for your mother. Pray for the doctors and the hospital. Pray for my will to be done on earth as it is in heaven."

I would fall to my knees again, asking for healing, and the answer would echo through me, "I am the resurrection and the life. He who believes in me will live, even though he dies; and whoever lives and believes in me will never die. Do you believe this?" And then he said, "Brenda, develop a heart of compassion for those who hurt and struggle in this world. Let your heart be moved by what moves mine. Have no fear, I am at work."

But this is my mother.

I would cry out again for favor and healing for her. And receive the reply, "Everyone will be salted with fire. Pray, so that you don't fall into temptation."

We wrestled.

I had experienced God's miraculous healing in answer to prayer before. God had healed a teenager I, and others, had prayed for when he was shot in the head by his father in an attempted murder-suicide. God had healed a pilot who had barely survived when his helicopter fell out of the sky shortly after take-off. The other people on board perished. He even healed my mother's dog when there was no hope, and restored my cat's eyesight when she was blinded. And now, why not my mother?

A friend suggested I buy a copy of *Jesus Calling* and send it to my mother as an encouragement for her. Before I put it in the mail, I turned to the devotional for that day, May 19. The reading stopped me cold. The following sentences, in particular, grabbed me: "You are on your way to heaven; nothing can prevent you from reaching that destination"[3] and "I will walk with you till the end of time, and onward into eternity."[4] I didn't want to believe that this time could be very soon for my mother, much sooner than I ever wanted it to be. My denial was strong that God might be taking my mother home. Looking back, I think that on a subconscious level I knew that was the case, but on a conscious level I didn't want to accept it. I wanted the outcome of this situation to be different.

I prayed again, and again God said to me, "Brenda, I know what you need and what your mother needs before you even ask me. Be assured. Pray for my name to be hallowed in your mother's circumstances. Pray for my kingdom to come on earth and for my will to be done on earth as it is in heaven. And forgive. Pray, so that you do not fall into temptation."

Had I prayed that I would not fall into temptation? No, not really. My prayers were for my mother, for her safekeeping, for her healing, for the dreams I had for us.

And now here I was, less than two months later, in a little thatched cottage in the mountains of the Free State. Since then, I had experienced my mother's death, witnessed the nursing staff's lack of regard for her, spoken at her funeral, watched as her white coffin was driven away, sorted through her clothes and personal effects, and gone through her kitchen cupboards.

I was in shock. Michiel went out on hikes and I sat in the warm winter sun to read. I had taken the book *God on Mute: Engaging the Silence of Unanswered Prayer* by Pete Greig off the bookshelves in the communal living room at the Farm. The following excerpt from the book spoke to me so clearly that I wrote it out in my journal:

> But we know that there is an anointing—an authority—that
> can only come to us through the darker trust of unanswered

prayer. It is an illumination both in us and through us that can only come through suffering; a healing that we can only minister when we ourselves have been wounded.[5]

God had said no to me. I had wrestled with him and he had wounded me; he had broken my heart like it had never been broken before.

I scribbled these words on the inside cover of my journal:

There is a change that comes only from a deep wounding.

There are some wounds that are so deep that, long after they have healed, there is still evidence of them: a scar, a limp, an amputation. This was my loss. I knew that I would never be the same again. My life would be divided into two sections: Brenda before Mom died, and Brenda after Mom died. And what would the Brenda after look like? Who would that Brenda be? How would this Brenda respond to the deep wounding, to this breaking of her heart? Would this be, as Tolkien called it, a *eucatastrophe* in her life?

I was introduced to this beautiful and powerful word and its meaning by Ann Voskamp in her book, *One Thousand Gifts*.

*Eucatastroph*e, coined by writer J.R.R. Tolkien, is the joining of the word Eucharist with the word catastrophe. In Christian liturgy, the Eucharist commemorates Jesus' last supper with his disciples before his crucifixion. It is a ceremony in which bread and wine are blessed and consumed, just as Jesus did at that last supper. As it is done to remember Jesus and his death on the cross, it is both an action of remembrance and of thanksgiving to God for reconciling us to himself through Jesus.

Eucatastrophe is the joining of thanksgiving to God with the catastrophes in our lives. It is this union that forges our characters into the likeness of Christ: we submit to God with thankful hearts, and, in turn, he redeems our suffering and gives us hope. Mom's death was my catastrophe. It was traumatizing, shocking, devastating, and faith-testing. The dream of the horse, staring at me face-to-face, was the challenge of the Eucharist. The challenge of giving thanks to God.

I had choices before me. The catastrophe was a done deal; nothing was going to change it now. But would I, in faith, live with a grateful heart, trusting God when, right now, there seemed no evidence of his goodness and his promises in my catastrophe? Would I let the Eucharist break through? Could I?

God would allow me to choose, like he always does, but his counsel to me, based on Deuteronomy 30:19-20, was this: "*Choose life and blessings: love the Lord your God; listen to his voice, and hold fast to him. For the Lord is your life.*"

CHAPTER SEVEN

I t was through my red-bound Children's Bible that God first prepared me to understand two things I would need to draw on to navigate this painful experience of my mother's death and neglect. The first is that he is a wild God who will not be domesticated, and the second is that the world is not safe. Our Children's Bible was letter size; one side of the page had a story while the other had a picture illustrating the story. Three stories stick most in my mind because of the pictures. They are the stories of Moses and the Ten Commandments, Elijah being taken up into heaven, and the beheading of John the Baptist.

The picture of Moses after he had received the Ten Commandments was full of raw energy and anger. He had come down the mountain to find that the Israelites had created a golden calf. The picture was of that moment when Moses, in fury and anger, raised the tablets above his head and was about to throw them to the ground in rage at the Israelites' wrongdoing. There was nothing placid or vanilla about that picture. It was all unadulterated emotion and anger at his people's deviance.

The picture depicting Elijah was one of energy as well, but also vibrancy. It was of that moment when the horses and chariot, made of fire, came between Elijah and Elisha. Elijah was in the chariot with the horses straining in their quest to take him heavenward. Elisha was likely in the picture with Elijah's coat on the ground. I don't remember exactly, because I would always feast my eyes on Elijah, on the powerful, determined horses, and on the brilliance of God that he would swoop down like that to take one of his prophets home.

As a child, I couldn't quite comprehend or articulate what the pictures in my Bible taught me. But looking back, I think the teaching was subconscious. The picture of Moses taught me that emotion is part of our life experience and that anger is a valid emotion. It also taught me that it is not right to disobey God and go your own way. God places high value on obedience. The depiction of Elijah taught me that God has some brilliant and out-of-this-world plans and that we don't all get the same treatment. Elijah was taken up in a chariot of fire, Elisha was left behind. Elijah was spared a mortal death, Elisha was not.

The third defining picture was of John the Baptist's head on a platter. Although that might be a strange picture to have in a children's Bible, I am glad it was in mine. The energy in that picture was in the movement of the platter as it was brought into the room. John the Baptist's severed, motionless head was a clear declaration that being a follower of Jesus and a lover of God can get you killed. I am always concerned at teachings that give a message of come to Jesus and be safe. Come to Jesus and have a life of comfort where everything falls into place. My experience is different from those messages. My experience and belief are rather: Come to Jesus. He is truth. He is the way to a life of purpose and meaning. He is the life worth living. Expect nothing less than an exciting and unpredictable ride that isn't first about your safety and comfort, it's about your personal transformation into his likeness and extending his Kingdom in a lost world that is at odds with him. And it comes at a price. But come, shrinking violets and warrior spirits. Come one and all; come and know what it is to truly live!

And in those small ways, through my red-bound Children's Bible, God started to instill that in me while I was still a child.

I grew up loving God and wanting to please him. I loved attending catechism and I certainly loved my first catechism teacher, Mrs. Toach. She increased my love for God and she taught me to pray. I loved going to church on Sundays with Mom and my brothers. I loved the black and white tiles of the church floor. I loved the quiet click of our heels as we walked up the aisle to a pew near the front of the church. I loved the stillness, the quietness, and kneeling to pray on the hard bench. I loved the pictures in the stained glass windows and the Stations of the Cross depicted on the walls. I loved the celebration of Mass. I loved to sing the hymns, especially after communion when Mom and I would kneel together and sing. And many times we would sing the last hymn in the car on the way home. I came to know and love God the Father through this.

I knew that Jesus had been crucified, that he died and rose on the third day. I knew that being a Christian was about Jesus, and that I should live my life forgiving others and being kind and considerate. I should not break the law. I should obey my parents. I should pray and be good.

When I was thirteen, the Gideons came to my high school. They did a presentation from the front of the school hall telling us about the Good News of Jesus Christ. We all received a small green New Testament. At home, I read the sinner's prayer that was written in the front pages. I decided to say the words out loud, declaring them to God, and wrote the date in the space provided, April 22, 1980.

Thereafter, as a teenager, I often read my Bible at night before bed. I wasn't a perfect teenager, but I wasn't rebellious either. I loved my mother and lived with the great tension that I disliked my father. In my Grade 12 year, the Redemptorist Priests came to our church for a week of teaching. Even though I was close to writing my mid-year exams, I attended the evening services every night that week. And on the Saturday, I went to confession where I cried and broke open my heart to the priest over my feelings towards my father.

The confessional was set up as an additional one to deal with the large number of people arriving for confession. It was in a small room with a curtain separating me and the priest. I knelt and started to confess my sins. I listed the usual ones, but I knew that I needed to do more than that. I had to do the hard work of naming my intense dislike for my father. And as I did, I started to cry and I couldn't stop. The priest reached around the curtain and brought me to sit in front of him, face to face. He spoke kindly to me. I don't recall what he said, but I know there was no condemnation, just love and understanding. And I was comforted.

That week in May 1984 was a defining week in my life. I was so deeply impacted by the Redemptorist teaching at our church and the care and love of that priest in the confessional that, if girls were allowed to be priests, I would have seriously considered joining the priesthood. Being a nun didn't appeal to me. I had a feminist streak and I didn't see why I should be a nun just because I was a woman. It was the priesthood that I felt drawn to, particularly preaching and shepherding.

The most striking message I heard that week, and one that I have remembered and drawn on since, is the realization that I am going to die. On one of the last evenings, the priest giving the message shared with the congregation that he was dying. My heart went out to him in sympathy. I wondered what illness he had. How long did he have to live? When did he find out? My concern for him was from a distance as I was young and healthy. I wasn't sick. I had my life in front of me. Dying was certainly not something I had to trouble myself with.

The turning point came when he disclosed the cause of his dying: he was alive. There was no illness, no sickness that was robbing him of his life and taking him towards his grave. He was headed towards his grave simply because of the fact that he was alive. At the age of seventeen, it struck me that dying doesn't just happen to other people, it will happen to me too. The gravity hit home; I was born to die. There in five words was the basic structure of my life. From the moment of my birth, I was both living and dying. My understanding of life was turned on its head that day.

For so many of us, we suppress thoughts of our own death and, in our denial, we try to live life to the full. However, we are living life to the full from a place of fear—afraid of death, afraid to talk about it, afraid to confront it and accept that it is part of living. We ignore it and pretend that it is not going to happen. At the age of seventeen, the reality of my death being the culminating event of my life seeped into my consciousness. I didn't live my life with perfect purpose and clarity after that. In fact, I made some poor choices, as many teens and young adults do. I also forgot about it for a number of years, but the seed was planted. And all those seeds planted in my childhood and youth were ones I would remember and draw on as I grieved my mother.

CHAPTER EIGHT

In August, a month after we returned to Vancouver from South Africa, I felt God stir in my heart and direct me to take the book *Secrets of the Vine* by Bruce Wilkinson off my bookshelf. Having read this book before, I knew that it would be relevant to the deep cutting and pruning God was doing in my life through the death of my mother. Using John 15, Bruce Wilkinson explores what it means for us, the branches, to abide in Jesus who is the vine. Wilkinson explains how God the Father prunes us for one of three reasons: either for discipline, or to bear more fruit, or to go deeper in our relationship with him. The purpose of the pruning is an indicator of its severity. He explains that "mature branches must be pruned hard to achieve maximum yields."[6] He writes too that "mature pruning is about your values and personal identity... What God asks of you now may seem difficult. But the results, if you say yes to the Vinedresser, will be dramatically more than you could have imagined."[7]

And then the caveat.

"Many Christians never get this far. In fact, if you're not really committed to reaching the next level of abundance—*more* fruit—you probably shouldn't read this chapter. When Jesus told His friends what it would cost to follow Him, many turned back."[8]

I held that little book in my hands and wondered, would I turn back? This pruning was indeed severe. So severe that my heart bled.

So severe that I questioned if Jesus was worth following. I wanted to turn back; I wanted to be free to be angry at God and hold someone responsible. I wanted to be bitter.

Questions raged in my head. Who needs a God like this anyway? Why follow a God who sends one of his faithful to die a hard death, a death she didn't deserve, at the hands of medical staff who didn't care a jot for her? Her lifetime of faithfulness to him, to her husband, to her children and grandsons earns her this? Really? Is this a just and fair reward?

I deeply questioned the truth of my faith. Is Jesus real? Is what has been said and written about him true? Does it even matter? Is heaven real? Or is it just make-believe? Does it even matter? Is this life of faith worth it? Why live at all? Why not just die, here, now? Death is the only guarantee after we are born. We are born to die, so why not end it now? Let's just be done with this façade we call life. God doesn't really care anyhow. He sits on his hands or is out playing golf when you need him the most. He's like police officers; where are they when you need them? Getting a Starbucks coffee.

My anger built.

I turned to the Book of Job. I knew that I had to. I had to try to make sense of my mother's death if I was going to have any true faith at all. I was grappling with the questions of Job: Why do the faithful suffer? Why do bad things happen to good people? Why bother pursuing goodness? Do unto others as you would have them do unto you. Really? And when you are kind and compassionate, abounding in love as my mother was, why wasn't she treated likewise in return? Especially by the medical staff. Don't they take the Hippocratic Oath? Apparently, it no longer has any weight. It should be renamed the Hypocritic Oath. The nursing staff didn't seem compelled to work by a code of ethics. So why not live for yourself? Others do. Why not just do what suits you, regardless of what it looks like. Take care of yourself. No one else is going to do it, especially not the medical staff. For the nurses, it is just a job to pay the bills; they aren't there to care for the sick and dying out of compassion. And for doctors, it is a get-rich industry; they care for those who can afford to pay them handsomely.

The anger and cynicism churned in me. The questions were a tempest in my mind and soul. The trauma of my mother's death was profound. A winter of depression overtook me.

I didn't find the way forward on my own, how could I? God guided me with crumbs in the snow. A crumb here and a crumb there to feed me and to illuminate my thoughts enough to stop them from shutting down completely or going in the wrong direction. He illuminated all that raged inside of me; he did not rescue me from any of it.

So often we want God to rescue us from our suffering the same way that he took Elijah up into heaven, with a great swoop of a heavenly chariot. There, done and dusted, no more suffering. We want to become spiritually mature the easy way, by osmosis, with as little discomfort as possible. We don't want to go into the wilderness; we want to by-pass it but still attain all its benefits. God in his wisdom did not rescue me from my questioning, from my soul-searching, from my devastation. Instead, he used it to prepare the soil of my life for a deeper and more genuine relationship with him. He used it to burn away the excesses of my life and strip me down to the bare essentials. And he left crumbs in the snow for me to follow, words of guidance from my Christian brothers and sisters and his own words to me in the Bible.

The introduction to the Book of Job in my NIV Bible was one of those crumbs in the snow. It explained that the Book of Job provides

> ...a profound statement on the subject of theodicy (the justice of God in the light of human suffering), and even more particularly, the suffering of the innocent. Those whose godliness is genuine, whose moral character is upright and who, though not sinless, have kept themselves from great transgression, but who nonetheless were made to suffer bitterly.[9]

That was my mother. A godly woman of moral character who, though not sinless, had kept herself from great transgression, yet was made to suffer bitterly. The introduction to the Book of Job went on to describe what was happening between me and God:

> The great adversary... as tempter he seeks to alienate man from God, as accuser he seeks to alienate God from man. His all-consuming purpose is to drive an irremovable wedge between God and man, to effect an alienation that cannot be reconciled.[10]

Those words exposed Satan's behind-the-scenes work. Through the actions of the medical staff, through the neglect and lack of care Mom suffered at the hospital, Satan was attempting to alienate me from God and drive an irremovable wedge between us, to create such a breakdown in our relationship that there could be no reconciliation.

I had seen others walk away from their faith. I had seen how disappointments and heartbreaks had caused them to question God, question his purpose and goodness, question why he had not come through for them in the way they had expected or hoped for, and they had walked away.

Now, with Satan's intentions exposed, I knew that I would not allow him to come between me and God. God and I still had some talking to do, but this would not break my faith. I decided instead to defeat Satan at his own game. I made the conscious choice to choose God, to trust God implicitly even though it hurt so badly I wanted to strike out at someone, and at someone who could've and should've made a difference: God himself.

Again the author of the introduction to Job had this pastoral word to say to me about the godly sufferer, my mother, that her,

> ...righteousness has such supreme value that God treasures it more than all. And the great adversary knows that if he is to thwart the purposes of God he must assail the righteousness of man. At stake in the suffering of the truly godly is the outcome of the struggle in heaven between the great adversary and God, with the all-encompassing divine purpose in the balance. Thus the suffering of the righteous has a meaning and a value commensurate with the titanic spiritual struggle of the ages.[11]

My mother's suffering was valued by God and it had a purpose, one that I could not see or understand. I could only trust by faith. Satan had been working in her situation to turn her against God but, although anguished by her illness, she did not turn against him. "*Though He smite me, still will I trust Him*" (Job 13:15). And now Satan was doing the same through my heartbreak and grief. In faith then, I chose to trust God and to walk by faith that he would lead the way through this intense grief. I chose to trust that all suffering can make us more like Christ. I chose to trust that he would use all things for the good of those who love him, know him, and are called according to his purpose.

As I sat at my desk one morning processing my grief, asking my questions, thinking and praying, my eyes fell on a thank you card that I had put in a frame and placed next to my desk. The picture, a drawing of a chandelier with balloons, ornaments, tinsel, stars, and flowers hanging from it, was festive, cheerful. The chandelier was white, etched in black, and the festive ornaments were glittering red, hues of pink, and bright blue against a neutral backdrop. I looked at it and through it while thoughts moved in my mind. I looked and I thought. And then I looked closer; the picture was upside-down. How had I never noticed that before? I reached for it and turned it the other way around. Yep! That was the right way. The ornaments now hung down from the chandelier. I turned the picture upside-down again and the festive ornaments defied gravity as they leapt and danced above the chandelier. The picture was certainly more vital and vibrant upside-down. It was more alive than the right way around. And then I heard this still small voice say to me, "See, Brenda, isn't it more beautiful? Isn't it more vibrant? I am the upside-down God. Trust me."

My life was now upside-down, my mother's death was upside-down. The circumstances of her death should never have played out as they did. Where was the purpose in her suffering? I may never know, but God was telling me to trust that he would make something beautiful and vibrant out of it. I responded in my journal with these words:

> Oh God, you have ripped my heart out of my chest. You have broken my heart with what breaks yours. Satan has intended

it for ill, but you intended it for good. You are my upside-down God. In you I trust. Continue your love and your righteousness to me (Psalm 36:10). Lord, you are the only true God. You are my God forever and ever; you will be my guide—today, tomorrow and every day—even to the end (Psalm 48:14).

And God answered, "Talk to me and see what I will do with your heartache—in you and in this world. You are right—I am the great Redeemer and I will turn your mother's suffering and neglect around to serve my purpose. Watch and wait—but don't expect to understand it and don't expect that it will look the way you want it to look. I am unfathomable; you will find peace if you live with this mystery, this tension. I am the upside-down God. Your picture of the chandelier, upside-down in its frame, is to remind you that I am the upside-down God. Doesn't it look more beautiful? Keep talking, keep listening, keep close. I will instruct you and teach you in the way that you should go."

I was comforted that day and every time I looked at the picture of the upside-down chandelier, yet I remained restless in my grief; it was still so new and raw. My grief was profound, my depression was overwhelming. But I had to function in my job; I had to keep putting one foot in front of the other. And my trust—it was still only in my head; it needed to reach my heart. I still anguished at what I saw as God's absence in the unfolding of the events in my mother's life and subsequent death.

Where, oh where are you God? Where were you as my mother lay in pain struggling for each breath when those who should have cared most for her were apathetic? When funds that should have been directed to her care and the care of others were siphoned off by those in power to pay for bigger swimming pools, glamorous clothes, and so-called business trips with lavish expense accounts, or even a personal estate? Where were you when doctors were not giving us the whole picture, but confusing us with false words of hope? Hope for what? A miraculous recovery when the truth was obviously the opposite, thereby robbing us of the advice and opportunity to make the right choices for our loved one?

"Where, oh God, are you in all this?" I cried to him.

"Right there, Brenda, sending your mother to the front lines to fight her last battle for me. Sending her to the front lines to expose that apathy, to expose the lack of funds, to expose the hatred and the anger, to expose the difficult conditions the doctors and nurses have to work with, to train you in the way you should go, to redefine your priorities, your focus, your heart. To expose you: to see what choices you will make, the path you will choose. Will you continue to follow me into the black night of suffering, or will you turn back? Will you go deeper in trusting me, or will the ground of your heart harden? I am right there, Brenda. The battle is not over, the battle is mine and I have a part for you to play. Are you willing? Are you up to it? If so, my training is not for the faint of heart. Come closer, come to me, sit with me, trust me, choose me and rest in me. Counter-intuitive? Yes, but when you do these things, you slay the plans of the evil one and the victory is mine."

Still I could not let it go and trust God. Still I churned inside with anger. Then I read these verses from 1 Peter 5:6-7: "*Humble yourselves, therefore, under God's mighty hand, that he may lift you up in due time. Cast all your anxiety on him because he cares for you.*"

These two verses brought about a turning point in my grief. In my quiet time of seeking understanding from God and of God, he had spoken. It was time for me to rest in him during my grief, my angst and confusion—to sit in it and embrace it, to no longer rail against it. As wrong as it all felt, God was in control, and it was time for me to humble myself at the outcome and to stop fighting it. God had allowed this suffering for me, for my mother, for my family. Suffering is part of God's way for us. How can it not be when we live in a fallen and depraved world? How can it not be when we are influenced by the actions and choices of others and they by ours? How can it not be when this world is marked by self-centeredness, selfishness, egos, individualism, anger, frustration, and deep hurt? We forget that we are living in a world that is at war. A world in which Satan is in strong opposition to the Lord of the universe. It is masked by the hum-drum of our lives, by the demands of making ends meet. We forget—and that is one of Satan's greatest assets. But then God bursts in with a reminder, a painful reminder that shakes us out of our reverie. And in response, we want answers.

Now though, I chose to leave the questions unanswered as I wrote words in my journal inspired by 1 Peter 5:1-11:

> Humble yourself under God's mighty hand that he may lift you up in due time. Cast all your sorrow and anxiety on him because he cares for you. You do not know the ways of the Almighty God. Humble yourself under his decisions and the path of suffering. Christ himself was familiar with suffering—a man of sorrows. In God's appointed time, just as Christ suffered and entered into glory, so all his people—including me and my mother—after their sufferings, will participate in his glory. And the God of all grace, who called you to his eternal glory in Christ, after you have suffered a little while, will himself restore you and make you strong, firm and steadfast.

I chose to rest and to sit in the pain of my grief, to submit myself under his mighty hand, knowing that he would use this time to prepare me for the time when he would lift me up. Often over the next weeks and months, I repeated a personalized version of the verses that had impacted me so greatly, "Brenda, humble yourself under God's mighty hand, that he may lift you up in due time. Cast all your anxiety on him because he cares for you."

CHAPTER
NINE

During this time of sitting in my pain, Bruce Wilkinson's explanations of a test of faith and of mature pruning instilled courage and perseverance in me.

Wilkinson described a test of faith as being a trial or hardship where I am being invited "to surrender something of great value to God *even when I had every right not to.*"[12] For me this was my mother. But this surrender, according to Wilkinson, is not pointless, it is not just a taking away, it is part of mature pruning where "God's shears cut closer to the core of who I am"[13] with the intent of adding "strength, productivity, and spiritual power in my life."[14] Wilkinson's explanation echoes words found in the Psalms:

For you, God, tested us;
you refined us like silver.
You brought us into prison
and laid burdens on our backs.
You let people ride over our heads;
we went through fire and water,
but you brought us to a place of abundance.
(Psalm 66:10-12)

These statements comforted me in my pain and reinforced the understanding I had of my dream of the horse, that God was saying, "Brenda, how you respond to your mother's death will determine how much more of my strength and power I will give you, and how I use you in the future." I was at a crossroads in my faith and how I responded was crucial.

I had previously wondered how solid mature Christians could sometimes walk away from their faith. They've worked in ministry. They've gone overseas on mission. They have been examples in the church to their brothers and sisters. And, one day, something shifts in them and they choose to turn away. Now I think I know. When you have lived your life for the Lord, when you have loved him and kept yourself for him, when you have risked for him and reached out to others for him, there seeps into the psyche an expectation of repayment in some way, some sense of favor. If not for us, at least for our loved ones. And when he doesn't grant us favor, our hurt is so great, we walk away. That's what it felt like for me. God had disappointed me deeply and my choice was this: walk away or walk deeper into the cold dark night with him, with no expectation of an answer.

"Who has given so much to God that God should repay him? Who has known the mind of the Lord? Or who has been his counselor?" (Romans 11:34-35)

Even as I tried to sit in my pain, my anger and confusion would rise to the surface: "God, you have broken my heart—you have ripped it out of my chest—and I am in shock and disbelief, at the experience, at the loss, and at what I have seen."

I struggled with understanding and accepting the injustice done to my mother, yet, while still not knowing, not understanding, I knew that there was only one choice I could make if I was to come out of this experience spiritually alive. I needed to follow Jesus into the dark. I needed to do what Bruce Wilkinson had advised during this time of shifting priorities: "God doesn't want me to do more *for* Him. He wants me to be more *with* Him."[15]

Abide.

The weeks and months that followed were a combination of keeping going and resting. *Keep going.* Those were the words with which Mark exhorted our mother as she lay nailed to her death bed. *Keep going.* They became words I spoke to myself as I put one foot in front of the other and navigated my way through my grief and depression. My morning quiet time became a precious time to me. My little room where I met with the Lord became hallowed ground as I prayed, read his word, and wrote in my journal. Many times I would just sit with my cup of tea in the quiet dark of the morning.

My journal is filled with God's words of encouragement to me, with our dialogues, and with insights I gained from the books God directed me to read. I have read Erwin McManus's *The Barbarian Way* many times, particularly during difficult times in my life. And in questioning my faith, I focused again on these excerpts from the book:

"A question we should all ask: If Jesus is not the one, we should not follow Him. But if He is the one, we should follow Him at all costs."[16]

And: "Jesus' purpose is to save us not from pain and suffering, but from meaninglessness. For Jesus, John the Baptist (in prison about to be executed) was exactly where he needed to be, fulfilling God's purpose for his life."[17]

And so was my mother. And so am I.

In my heart it wasn't what I wanted to hear or believe. The only way I could embrace those words was to tap into God's perspective and his heart for the world. Using words from McManus's writing, I wrote this request of God in my journal:

"Let my heart beat 'to the rhythm of the heart of God.'"[18]

And he responded: "Blessed are you, Brenda, if you do not fall away on account of me (Matthew 11:6). I, Jesus, am the author and the perfecter of your faith. I am in the process of doing that right now as you grapple with the grief of your mother's death. I discipline and train you, prune you for your good that you may share in my holiness. No pruning seems pleasant at the time, but painful. Later on, however, it produces a harvest of righteousness and peace for those who have been trained by it. Therefore, strengthen your feeble arms and weak knees.

Make level paths for your feet, so that the lame may not be disabled, but rather healed" (Hebrews 12:2, 10b-12).

Our conversation continued:

Praise be to you the God and Father of my Lord Jesus Christ, the Father of compassion and the God of all comfort, who comforts me in all my troubles and grief, so that I can comfort those in any trouble with the comfort I myself have received from God. For just as the sufferings of Christ and the evil of this world flow over into my life, so also through Christ my comfort overflows (2 Corinthians 1:3-6).

"Brenda, do not be surprised at the painful trial you are suffering, as though something strange were happening to you. But rejoice that you participate in the sufferings of Christ, so that you may be overjoyed when his glory is revealed. So then, now that you suffer according to God's will, commit yourself to your faithful Creator and continue to do good" (1 Peter 4:12, 13, 19).

My concluding response was paraphrased from Psalm 116, verses 16 and 7:

"O Lord, truly I am your servant; I am your servant, the daughter of your maidservant; Be at rest once more, O my soul, for the Lord has been good to you."

When we abide in the Lord, we come to exude a rest and beauty that is not our own.

At church one Sunday, a friend greeted me with a warm hug. As she hugged me, she murmured in my ear, "You look so beautiful and peaceful. You are glowing."

"Oh, Melanie," I replied, "that isn't how I feel. I'm emotionally wrecked. I am so broken inside I can hardly go on."

"Well, you are beautiful in your rawness," she responded.

On another occasion at church, I was getting a cup of tea just before going into one of my evening GriefShare sessions. I connected with a woman I knew, to some extent, who was coming out of a Board meeting.

"Brenda," she said, "you are looking so lovely and rested."

Rested? Really? I was resting in God, but not feeling rested. I was exhausted and fatigued by my grief. In my internal world I was still depressed and distressed. But I started to realize that what others were seeing was the Lord carrying me. I was encouraged that the Lord was indeed with me. When I received the third compliment, I knew better how to respond. Again at church, a friend spoke to me in the pews after the service.

"I must tell you," she said, "people are talking about you. They are saying, 'Have you seen Brenda Smit? She looks stunning and so peaceful'."

I thanked her and replied, "Debbie, it is the Lord that they are seeing. It is not me, I am too cut up inside for it to be me."

I was feeling broken and distraught, and yet my countenance was not reflecting my inner turmoil and my devastation. I was getting through each day one step and one moment at a time, and yet my countenance was one of peace and tranquility. That was surely a reflection of my abiding in the Lord. The Lord hemmed me in. He was in me, before me, behind me, and beside me. He filled my face with his glow.

CHAPTER
TEN

As close as I was to my mother, there was distance in my relationship with my father. Dad was not someone to let others get too close to him and that distance defined our relationship. That and the fact that I was a girl. Dad wasn't too sure about girls. Somewhere in his mind, girls were screamers, criers, and emotionally messy. Cowboys don't cry, and cowgirls? Well, they shouldn't cry either.

Although under the same roof, Dad and I lived a short distance from each other. The space between us was steeped in his thoughts and expectations of how I, as a girl, would be. In fairness, I also had thoughts and expectations of how he, as a father, should be. My father knew better how to relate to boys than girls. With a son he could kick a ball, coach soccer, and watch sports. But a girl?

I remember my Grandmother James telling me how, as a baby, my hair had curls. She would brush my hair and fluff up all my curls. If my father came into the room, he would take the brush and brush them all flat. Perhaps, in his mind, boys don't have wisps of curls floating on their heads like little halos.

Dad and I didn't know or understand each other for most of our lives. That is, until we spent two weeks together just before he died. I have no memories of Dad putting me on his lap, reading me bedtime stories (then again neither did Mom), holding my hand when we walked, comforting me, or giving me kisses. That I got from my mother.

One of my fondest family memories is winter Saturday mornings as a teen. I would get bundled up on those brisk winter mornings and head out with Dad and Mom to go and watch one of my brothers, Grant or Clinton, play rugby for Springs Boys High. I enjoyed the excitement, eyeing out the boys and shouting from the sidelines. And if that wasn't enough sport for the day, Saturday afternoons would be spent on the couch watching TopSport. I would watch it all: boxing, Formula 1 racing, golf, tennis, snooker, horse racing, the Duzi canoe marathon—you name it, I pretty much watched it.

I didn't realize it at the time, but that was how I connected with my father. Deep in me, as in all children, was a need to connect with and to love and be loved by my parents. I knew I was loved by my mother; we had a deep connection. But my father was a different story. I didn't always know or feel that my father loved me, so I found ways to be with him, to share his interests, to be acceptable to him, to have a bond. And it was sports. I wasn't a sportswoman by a long shot, so I watched sports. I came to know and understand the sports that Dad enjoyed: rugby, cricket, soccer.

Dad was not a demonstratively affectionate father and only once did I ever hear him say that he loved me. And, sadly, I received it as too little, too late.

I was nineteen, out of the house and living with my boyfriend. At my cousin's wedding, Dad asked me to dance with him. Although not drunk, Dad had, of course, been drinking. As we danced, he pulled me closer to him and said into my hair, "I love you". It would've meant more to me if Dad had whispered those words to me without any alcohol in him. But he didn't. And, at the time, I had no understanding that he couldn't.

I heard the words and said nothing. My body didn't respond in any way either. I didn't need him now. I didn't need his declaration of love. I had a boyfriend who told me what I wanted to hear. My love and acceptance came from another source; my father was now no one in my life. When the music finished, I walked off the dance floor without responding.

Our parents shape us, whether we like it or not. I liked to think that I stood outside of my father's influence, that I was nothing like him. I thought I was my own person who made my own decisions. I thought that once I removed myself from the close confines of life with my father, I would be free of the tension I felt towards him and I could go on with my life. And yet, at the same time, I knew that I was shaped by my love for my mother and her positive example. I have always felt a warm glow when I have been likened positively to her.

Shortly after Mom died, I was interacting with her gardener, Isaac. I gave him a guava, thinking he might appreciate something sweet and refreshing after a day's work in the garden. He duly tucked it away and explained he was taking it home to his two daughters.

"Well then, you need two," I said. And I gave him a second one. Next I gave him his wages, payment for the work he had done in the yard, and added a bonus.

He gladly received his wages, sincerely expressed his thanks for the bonus, and said to me, "You look like your mother. You sound like your mother. You are kind like your mother."

What a beautiful compliment to receive so shortly after my mother's difficult and unexpected death. It was a gift of treasure to me.

At my father's funeral, the organist who had also played at Mom's funeral, and who had known my mother for many years, commented to me, "You are so like your mother. I was watching you talk to someone. You have the same twinkling eyes."

I will treasure that comment and the gift of my twinkling eyes from my mother forever. Had I received both comments while my mother was still alive, I don't think those words would've found such fertile ground as they did after her death. There is a depth of love you can only tap into once a loved one has died.

Likewise, I have been paralleled to my father. However, the tribute was not nearly as gladly received. Within days of hearing of my father's death, I was in that sacrosanct confessional, my hairdresser's chair, sharing with him the experience of my recent trip to South Africa to visit my father, my interaction with Dad while I was there, and now his death.

"He is so stubborn," I said of my father.

"Just like you," my hairdresser replied.

I was not quite gob-smacked, but the comment did cause me to straighten in the chair. Stubborn? Me? My response was one of denial. "I'm not stubborn," I retorted. Then I faltered, "Am I?"

"Just a little," he confirmed.

The statement had been made and I didn't like it. I had a choice to make. I could continue in my denial and reject any statement that I am stubborn like my father and, in anger, lash out at anyone who would even suggest that I am. I could accept the lesser statement of 'just a little', thereby minimizing the comparison and relegating it to the pile of little consequence, so no change would be required. Or I could receive it, ponder it, and see myself through the eyes of my hairdresser. Even though he interacts with me just once every six weeks for an hour, he has experienced me as stubborn. I didn't like the stubbornness I saw in my father, why would I think it would look more pleasing in me?

Character development is a process. It is never complete. Once one layer is peeled off, there is another. But the upside of the process is that our egos get smaller with each layer that is removed. The reverse is also true. We can stop the process dead in its tracks with denial, anger, or addictions. When we do that, our egos get bigger, we protect ourselves with layers of blame and a hard shell, and we use attack as an additional means of defense.

For years I saw myself as having being formed by the best in my mother, believing that my father had little influence over me. As long as I didn't drink like he did, as long as I was kind like my mother, as long as my faith shaped me, and as long as I kept my distance from him, I wouldn't become like him. I would be better than he was.

It took forty years for the first layer of denial in my relationship with my father to be uncovered, and it took another decade for me to change. It took the death of my mother for me to see my father with new eyes and to further change my expectations of him. It took his death for me to recognize the positive aspects he contributed to my life.

PART TWO

DAD

This photo of Dad captures him so well, Christmas 2008,
in Springs, South Africa.

CHAPTER ELEVEN

For six months after Mom's death, I grieved deeply for her. At times I felt that I was barely surviving. My work was demanding and my heartache was great; my body ached with grief and work stress. Getting to the six-month anniversary of Mom's death was an accomplishment in itself.

After those six months of deep grief, God started to turn my attention to my father. Of my own, I was concerned for him and prayed for a difference in his life, but honestly, I also hoped that the problem would go away, and soon. God's plans were, again, different from mine. He intended to completely change my heart towards my father. He intended to heal me by transforming my heart, my mind, and my soul in my relationship with my father.

I didn't know how to relate to him. We didn't have much of a relationship to speak of. My relationship had always been with my mother. But now, with Mom gone, I was forced to interact with Dad— at least to some extent—without it being via a third party.

Phone calls to Dad were usually sporadic and with Michiel on the line, which made the calls easier for me. Dad liked Michiel and he had more to say to my husband than he did to me. Most times Dad would answer my greeting with a, "Yes, Miss Ann, what can I do for you?"

"Um, nothing, I'm just calling to say hello."

And so the conversation would die.

Questions about how things were or what was happening in his life would be met with, "I get up, I shower, I go to work, I have a few beers, I go to bed. That's my life."

Dad never asked about me at all. He might engage Michiel about life to some extent, and he might make a passing comment about the downside of life in South Africa, especially its regular power cuts. That invariably led to him saying that we had made the right decision to emigrate, and if we ever came back to live in South Africa he would kick us in the butt. Our conversations were typically very short, all of three minutes. Sometimes the conversations were better, and longer, and we'd feel good about them afterwards. But mostly not. Hence, I wasn't eager to call to say hello. In fact, I dreaded the calls.

I knew that Dad was lonely, probably very lonely, and I did feel for him. But really, it served him right. It was his own fault and he deserved it. He had created his own reality. He could have been kinder and more loving to Mom. The fact that he was now without his wife was part of his doing. He wasn't easy to live with. He had taken Mom for granted and hadn't appreciated her and all that she had done for him. *So now let's see how he likes it.*

As these thoughts stirred in me, I knew that my thoughts were not God's thoughts.

After Mom's death, Dad's drinking, which had previously been moderated by her presence, escalated. At first he started to drink more, and then he switched from drinking beer to drinking vodka and drank at least as much, and eventually more. In his grief, Dad was desperately lost. He was drinking away his sorrows and drowning in them too. Being so far away, I wasn't exposed to it, other than the reports I got from Mark, an occasional text of frustration from Tracy, my sister-in-law, and the odd phone conversation with Dad when he was obviously inebriated. Still, his drinking was a concern for all of us.

I had a deep sense that Dad was committing a slow suicide. He had no reason to live. He had never acquired the skills to navigate life and resolve personal problems. He had never explored and come to terms with his emotions. And so, when his emotions overwhelmed him in his grief, he did what he had always done, he drank them into submission. But his emotions were relentless. They would resurface and he would need to drink more. He was desperately lost and, with his support system in my mother gone, he was adrift with no way of knowing how to save himself. I prayed often that God would save him, that he would let God save him, that his life would turn around and that he would finish well. I prayed that he would know the love and joy that only God could give, the love and joy that was absent from his life.

In January 2015, God started to stir in me that I should reach out to Dad. First, it was a Sunday mission sermon from our pastor, Dave Sattler, during which he challenged the congregation to reach out to just one person who didn't know the Lord. Dad came to mind. This challenge was coupled with a testimony that was shared that Sunday.

The giver of the testimony, Jason, shared how he had been anti-God. A friend of his became a believer in Jesus and felt compelled to share the Good News of Christ with him. But knowing how anti-God Jason was, the friend needed courage to approach him. He arranged to meet with Jason, but before he arrived, Jason heard God say to him that his friend was coming to tell him about God, about Jesus. As a result, when his friend arrived and told Jason about Jesus, Jason said, "I know" and he accepted the Lord.

Jason's story encouraged me that God could already be preparing Dad to receive the message, I just needed to be faithful and obedient. However, like Jason's friend, I too needed courage to approach Dad.

Later in January, author and pastor Mark Buchanan came to preach at our church. His sermon was on the Good Samaritan. In his sermon, he posed the questions: Who is my neighbor? I am powerless to save myself, who will reach down and help lift me out of the ditch? Who am I a neighbor to?

Again, I thought of Dad. He was in the ditch of alcoholism with no hope. He was committing suicide: death by drink. It is a slow death, for the one dying and for those who are being deeply affected by it. As I processed all of this, I realized that my family's pattern of behavior was to step away from Dad and leave him to his own devices. He was volatile and hurtful. He was off-putting and swatted away care and concern. He could be callous and cantankerous. In no way did he even indicate that he wanted any help. But I knew that I needed to be the neighbor who reached out to Dad. I couldn't live with myself if I didn't. I needed to change my pattern of behavior of leaving him to his own devices. And so I came home after church, sat down, prayed, and wrote these words in a card for his upcoming birthday:

Dear Dad,

It seems empty to wish you a Happy Birthday at a time that has been very difficult for you and for all of us. Mom's passing has been one of the most difficult experiences I have ever had to journey through, very likely for you too. There have been times over the last six months the pain and grief have been difficult to bear and I have felt overwhelmed and lost. I am grateful for Michiel's support but most especially for my faith which has helped me to make sense of this pain and given me hope.

Without hope the heart perishes.

Rather than wish you a happy birthday, Dad, I wish you hope—a hope that enables you to carry on without Mom and rebuild a life that allows you to move forward and know joy. I wish you a hope that gives you purpose every day and a reason for living. I wish you a hope that enables you to finish well. I wish you everlasting and eternal hope. And that type of hope is only to be found in Jesus. There is no other hope that can rescue us.

Dad, the devil may look after his own (as you often say), but you do not belong to that deceiver, you belong to the God of the Universe who created you, who knows you by name and who loves you deeply. You are not alone. He is with you.

Dad, this birthday my hope for you is that you would call on Jesus to save you, to put your feet on firm ground and to lift you into the life that He has for you. You need only ask Him. You cannot find a hope for living in yourself, none of us can, not at a time like this, but you can find it in Him. My prayer for you is that you do.

> I love you, Dad!
> Your daughter always,
> Brenda

I realize now that writing that card was as much for me as for Dad. I needed to take that courageous step of obedience, regardless of the outcome. I needed to express my love to my father, the extent to which I didn't even realize I felt towards him. I hoped that my letter would be used to transform Dad. That on receiving it, he would fall on his knees, repent, and ask God to forgive him and live in him.

My card arrived and was received without an acknowledgement. There was no change. At least not outwardly. Dad continued on his trajectory of self-destruction. But in me there was a change; when I was obedient and wrote the card, God softened my heart toward Dad. I wrote this prayer for him in my journal (based on Matthew 13:15 and inspired by the book *Waking the Dead* by John Eldredge):

> For my father's heart has become calloused; he hardly hears with his ears. And he has closed his eyes. Lord, wake him from his sleep. Arise sleepwalker! Awake from the living dead, that you may see with your eyes, hear with your ears, understand with your heart, and turn and Jesus will heal you.

And still it was silent. There was no indication that Dad would change or slow down his drinking. In June, Dad consulted a doctor with regard to hemorrhoids. He needed surgery. In preparing Dad for surgery, they discovered that his blood pressure was dangerously high. Dad was hospitalized to get his blood pressure under control and instructed to take his medication and to stop drinking; his health was suffering. Dad refused. He would rather live with the pain and self-medicate with alcohol. I felt discouraged; the situation was devoid of hope. Why even bother? Why not just leave him to live life on his own?

The answer came: "... *for this man, too, is a son of Abraham. For the Son of Man came to seek and to save what was lost. How much more valuable is a man than a sheep?"* (Luke 19:9b-10 and Matthew 12:12)

God saw value in my father. Value that we, Dad's children, struggled to see.

I wrestled with my discouragement and concern for Dad. However, God was not absent in my discouragement. He encouraged me through the prophet Elijah. In 1 Kings 18:41-45, Elijah is praying for rain. He sends his servant out to look for evidence of any clouds. There is none. Elijah continues to pray and again sends his servant to look for evidence of any clouds. Still nothing. He does this seven times and only then is there a wisp of cloud on the horizon, just a wisp. God was encouraging me to persevere in praying for my father, even when there was no evidence of change.

During this time, God led me to take another book off my shelf, *Jesus Today: A Spirituality of Radical Freedom* by Albert Nolan. A gift from my brother Mark, and written by one of his Dominican brothers, it had been on my shelf for about six years. Now was the time to read it.

I was struck by a statement in the introduction: "On the whole we don't take Jesus seriously... by and large we don't love our enemies, we don't turn the other cheek, we don't forgive seventy times seven times, we don't bless those who curse us, we don't share what we have with the poor, and we don't put all our hope and trust in God."[19]

In reading just that opening statement, I knew that God had a journey in mind for me that was going to take me into an even deeper relationship with him. If I thought I had been on a deep enough journey with him since my mother's death, I was mistaken. There is no end to spiritual maturity, not this side of heaven. There is no end to God's deep love for me and his desire to transform me ever closer into the likeness of his Son. God had already shown me through my mother's death that he was the upside-down God. And now he was to show me how to take Jesus, the upside-down Messiah, seriously.

As a Christian, I knew that Jesus was fully God and fully man. But to some extent it was on a head level. The concept of looking closely at how Jesus, the man, practiced his spirituality so that I might imitate him was not something I had given thought to before. I knew that Jesus went out alone to pray and so should I. I knew that Jesus instructed me to forgive as I have been forgiven, and mostly I did, but at times I struggled to do so. I knew that Jesus was a role model, but really, to be honest, he was also God and so, surely, it would've been easier for him than it could possibly be for me. Albert Nolan's comment that not enough of us take Jesus seriously stirred me to my core. It was time for me to take Jesus seriously—period.

I determined to experience a closer and more intimate relationship with God the way Jesus had while on earth, and to learn to love all humankind the way God and Jesus did.

I might have had the expectation that Dad should change to be worthy of my love, but God and Jesus didn't. I might have thought that Dad was unlovable in his drunken state, but God and Jesus didn't. I might have thought that he shouldn't be forgiven for his choices and actions, but God and Jesus didn't. My love and forgiveness were conditional, God's isn't. Rather, God showed his love for all men, women, and children—irrespectively—by sending Christ to die for us while we were, and are, still enmeshed in our sin.

God's starting point is love. *"For God so loved the world, that he gave his one and only Son, that whoever believes in him shall not perish but have eternal life"* (John 3:16). My starting point was remorse and repentance: when my father changed, when he acknowledged his sin and his wrongdoing, when he said sorry, then, and only then, would I extend love and forgiveness to him.

Jesus saw and still sees people, including my father, as lost, as wounded and broken, as sick, confused, and afraid. He saw my father in need of healing. Could I do the same? Could I see my father as lost and love him with the same unconditional love with which Jesus loved him?

As Nolan writes, "Jesus' respect for the dignity of everyone he encountered was boundless. He treated each individual as unique and lovable... and important."[20]

Could I, like Jesus, treat my father with the respect I didn't always feel towards him? Could I trust God to meet my emotional needs, the ones that my earthly father had never filled? Could I release my father from my expectation that he fill them?

According to Nolan, "Jesus' attitude, his way of treating people, the attention he gave them, and the way he enjoyed meals with them no matter who they were or what they might have done, spoke louder than words."[21]

One of my Dad's sayings was that talk is cheap, and actions speak louder than words. Jesus demonstrated this. Could my love and care for my father speak like that, louder than words? Could I see my father as infinitely valuable, as Jesus did? Could I love my father without any imputation of guilt and condemnation?

Of my own, I knew that I couldn't.

My desire to be like Jesus, in ever-increasing measure, was on full alert. The example to follow had been laid before me. The challenge was to step into it and to experience God as *Abba*, the way Jesus did, by being, as Nolan described it, a person "frequently wrapped in prayer."[22]

Spending time with Jesus and crying out to God was not new to me. I had done that for a long time, most intensely the previous ten months through the journey of my mother's illness and death. I already knew God intimately, but a new way of living from my heart was needed. A living from my heart, out of my woundedness, in the bosom of the Trinity, with utter trust in God as faithful and loving, with all my senses tuned to him so that I could live and act according to his will.

John Eldredge described my challenge in *Waking the Dead*. In it, he describes how finding God involves a total commitment of the heart. It is from our heart that we love him, hear his voice, and remain present to him. As he puts it, "You cannot be the person God meant you to be, and you cannot live the life he meant you to live, unless you live from the heart."[23] However, "the story of your life is the story of the long and brutal assault on your heart by the one who knows what you could be and fears it."[24]

As the Bible says, *"Guard your heart, for it is the wellspring of life"* (Proverbs 4:23).

CHAPTER
TWELVE

My heart has been the most brutally assaulted by my father. All my life, I wanted to experience his love and acceptance. By my late teens, when my attempts to draw close to him and to be accepted by him were not reciprocated, I rejected him and declared that I did not need him in my life. But it was a lie.

Of all my earliest memories of my father, one always surfaces first.

Mom and I were sitting at the kitchen table in our house on Carey Street. She was helping me finish my artwork, a picture of a duck paddling along on the water. I had traced the duck from the one Miss Williams, my Grade One teacher, had given us for just that purpose. I added my own personal touches of the water it was paddling in, a sun in the sky, and a couple of birds flying by, standard additions for the juvenile artist in me. I had colored them in and now Mom was helping me paste pipe cleaners on the outline of the duck, the water, the sun, and the birds. Dad sat on a stool, leaning against the kitchen counter, sipping his beer and watching us.

Mom and I finished it. I held up my picture, proud of it.

Dad asked to see it. I hesitated.

Mom assured me, "It's okay. You can show Dad."

I gave my picture to my father for him to admire. He took it, looked at it for a moment, and then tore it in two. The picture of my duck fell to the floor. I was devastated. Mom was equally devastated. We cried bitterly together. There was no time to do another one. I don't think I could have, even if there had been time. The next day, instead of my picture, I took a note to school for my teacher.

I handed it to her and I felt my shame.

My father's drinking defined our family. I learned from a young age to watch for his car as it pulled into the driveway after work. I searched out his face as he drove in for evidence of drinking before he came home. Was he coming straight from work or had he knocked off early and stopped at the pub on the way? I looked for two distinct features, a certain smile he had when he had been drinking, and how he held one hand against his stomach when he walked up the path to the front door. If either or both of those characteristics were present, I knew to stay out of his way.

My parents had many arguments when Dad was drunk. He liked to stir things up and pick a fight. An early memory is sitting in the bath with my younger brother, Clinton, and hearing my parents argue in the kitchen. We sat. We didn't play. Unattended, we didn't make waves whooshing up and down the long bath as we were sometimes inclined to do. We sat and we listened. The bath water grew cold. I can still feel the tense atmosphere in the bathroom. The air was thick and still as it is with an approaching storm. The house quietened. Our parents' arguing stopped. Next, we heard my mother scream.

When we were teenagers, the drinking and fighting peaked and became more physical. My father would have been around forty years old, often a time of evaluation and regret. During that time, when speaking with my mother, I started to refer to my father as *your husband*. He wasn't a father I respected or wanted to claim as my own. There were times when he would come home late from drinking at the lawn bowling club and I would pray that he would have a single-car accident on the way home and die. I wanted to be free of him, and of the pain and discord he brought into our lives.

At the beginning of my Grade 12 year, we had a family gathering to celebrate an engagement. That night my father got increasingly drunk and disorderly. A fight broke out and Dad was involved, at least, if not the cause. I was embarrassed and ashamed. Furious, I informed my mother that if this type of behavior from my father was going to continue, I would move out and live somewhere else so that I could focus on my studies. Dad continued to drink. And I didn't move out. I should have, but I didn't. It would have been too much of a public declaration of the craziness going on at home. Four months later, when the Redemptorist priests visited our church, I cried my heart out in the confessional.

I find these memories difficult to write and am embarrassed at the thought of them. Our family life was far from perfect. I remember clearly Dad's motto: What happens at home stays at home. It was our vow of silence.

I longed to leave home. I longed for a life different from the one I lived with my parents. I did the next best thing; I lived phantom-like, hiding in my bedroom with the door closed. And I read voraciously. My bedroom was my refuge from the fighting and from watching my father drink. I coped by isolating myself. I escaped into reading, and day-dreaming.

If only I could get out, I would be okay, I thought. I could leave it all behind.

And get out I did, at the age of nineteen, straight into the arms of an alcoholic boyfriend.

You'd think that I would have run a mile from a man who drank. And it's not that I was conned. My boyfriend, Dan, did not hide his drinking from me, no, he drank openly and unashamedly. He sported it with pride. I have since learned that, until we recognize and deal with the hurts and the negative patterns of behavior in our lives, we perpetuate them. And to be fair to myself, although I didn't like his drinking, I did like the attention he paid me. He pursued me and, like a parched throat, I drank in his attention, never quite able to quench the thirst.

Dan filled the father-void of my heart. He gave me the attention my father didn't. And looking back, perhaps it was important to me that my boyfriend drank as proof that it was possible for someone who drinks to choose me. Did I rationalize all this at the age of eighteen, going on nineteen? No, I was young, immature, and desperate to be loved by a man. My low self-esteem didn't equip me to believe that I could possibly be worth more than fourteenth place behind a dozen beers and the narcissistic personality of the alcoholic. Not only did I date the alcoholic boyfriend, but I moved in with him, loved him, and married him.

Surprisingly, I was the one who asked him to marry me. Dan had asked me to marry him enough times in the five years before our wedding that he had stopped asking.

It was August 1990, a bright, sunny Johannesburg winter Sunday. Dan and I had bought a country house in need of repair earlier that year. His parents lived with us and they had started to attend the local Methodist Church just up the road.

His mother invited me to attend with them.

"The pastor is really very good," I remember her saying.

And he was. He was a Jew who had come to know Jesus and was eager to convey to his parishioners the life change that occurs when we commit fully to Jesus. We had been attending the church for a short while, with Dan's parents, when the pastor preached a sermon one Sunday that changed my life.

He spoke about making pastoral visits where he would arrive unannounced at the front door. It was not uncommon in South Africa at the time for visitors to pop in without calling first. Still, when he arrived unexpectedly at the front door, he could often hear a flurry of activity inside as the parishioners hurriedly tidied the house before they opened the front door.

Likewise, he went on to explain, Jesus knocks on the door of our lives and we hesitate to answer because our lives are in disarray. We want to first tidy up our lives, clean up our act, and get things straightened out before we let him in.

That resonated so strongly with me. I had been sensing God calling me back to my faith. The one I had left for the love of a boyfriend. But because we were living together, and because I didn't know how to leave and stay gone, I kept saying, "I'm coming back, Lord, I just need to sort this out first."

That Sunday, our pastor went on to explain that we don't have to sort out our lives first. In fact, we shouldn't. Because if we do, we will more than likely put things in the wrong place. This is exactly the time to open the door and let Jesus in because he will clean up the house of our lives and put everything in its right and proper place.

That was the message I needed to hear.

Our pastor ended with a prayer and, while our heads were bowed, he asked all of those who would like to ask Jesus into their lives that Sunday to stand. I desperately wanted to stand but I didn't dare. I didn't know what Dan might think of that and I didn't want to face his wrath.

So I remained seated and silently prayed, *Lord, you know I want to stand, but I just can't. Please come into my life and put things into their right and proper place. You know I have tried, but I just can't get it right.*

I had known and loved God since I was a child. But it was in this little country Methodist Church that the final piece of the puzzle fitted. Jesus wasn't just an addendum to my life, he was my life.

After church, as I was washing the dishes, I had a chat with Jesus. I knew that I wanted out of the relationship. I loved Dan, but I also knew that this relationship wasn't really what I wanted. I asked Jesus to show me the way. And I told him that if he wanted me to marry my boyfriend, he would have to change my heart.

At the end of September, we had an almighty fight. I was pretty sure that it would end our relationship, that Jesus was showing me a way out, and that I would be on my way. But none of that materialized. Our relationship didn't end, Jesus didn't show me a way out, and I didn't leave. After that fight, things settled down between us. And slowly I felt my heart towards Dan change.

Increasingly, I felt that we should get married. Late in January 1991, I asked him if he would marry me. He was skeptical at first, given all my previous rebuffs of marriage. We spoke some more. He realized that I was serious and he agreed. We got engaged in February 1991 and we married six weeks later.

My husband was nine years older than I was. He was charming with a controlling personality. Over the years, his reins of control got tighter and tighter. Our marriage did not cause him to loosen his control of me. It stayed as tight as ever. He told me what I could wear, when I could cut my hair, if I could go out, and who my friends could be. In due course I had no friends, no key for my own front door, and, for the most part, I didn't leave home without being in his company or that of his parents. But at least he paid attention to me and, although I didn't like his control of my life, I mistakenly saw it as an expression of love for me.

Our relationship and marriage were volatile. We fought a lot, and when things were bad, they were really bad. There were many times that it was good and then it was really good, but it could change like the wind.

Two years after our wedding, during a difficult time in his life and our marriage, I awoke on a cold winter July morning to find that Dan had committed suicide. I felt betrayed. On our wedding day, he had promised me that he would always love me and be there for me. And now he wasn't.

I was twenty-six years old. I inherited some debt, a country house in need of repair on two and a half acres of land, five dogs, two cats, and little else.

The year of his death, I had managed to convince Dan to let me return to university to study for my post-graduate teaching diploma. Consequently, I was outside of his control and line of sight from the time he dropped me at university for my classes until he picked me up at the end of my day. That created tension in our marriage. His unemployment didn't help matters as I had somewhere to go every day and he did not.

We had also been trying to conceive a child with no success. And there was another emotional strain. Since our wedding day, he had experienced an estranged relationship with his young daughters from his first marriage. It all proved too much for him. One night, under the influence of depression and alcohol, he took his own life.

Financially, I was in a serious situation. We were already living in debt and I had no means to pay for the remainder of my education. Thankfully, a grant from the University of the Witwatersrand paid the remainder of my tuition fees and, with financial assistance from different family members, I was able to finish my year of study.

The following year I found employment as a secondary school teacher and started to rebuild my life. But I was done with marriage and relationships. From what I had seen and experienced of both, I didn't need either. I made a personal vow to remain single for the rest of my life. I would not let another man break my heart.

But God had a different plan for me.

First, he let me know that he had another husband in mind for me.

After my husband's death, the small community at my Methodist Church embraced me and took me into their fold. I started to attend a Bible study group comprised of adults in their fifties and sixties. These were godly men and women who cared for me, watched out for me, and helped me navigate the waters of wrapping up an estate.

One night, I didn't feel like going out to attend my small group. It was winter and a year since my husband's suicide. It was cold, it was dark, and I was depressed. But I knew that if I didn't go, I would receive a phone call from someone enquiring after me. I sighed. I placed one foot in front of the other. I put on my coat and I went.

That evening a woman attended who was a guest in the group as she was visiting the host couple. I was noticeably depressed and contributed little to the discussion. At the end of the evening, the guest told me that she had two passages from the Bible she believed God had given her to share with me. They were Isaiah 54:1-5 and Jeremiah 29:11-13. She encouraged me to see God as my husband and provider and to seek God in prayer.

That evening I went home, knelt by my bedside, and turned to the book of Jeremiah. I read the passage, which was new to me at the time.

> "'For I know the plans I have for you,' declares the Lord, 'plans to prosper you and not to harm you, plans to give you a hope and a future. Then you will call upon me and come and pray to me, and I will listen to you. You will seek me and find me when you seek me with all your heart'" (Jeremiah 29:11-13).

Jeremiah's mandate to call upon the Lord and to come and pray to him resonated with me as I was not talking to God at that point. I wasn't angry with him, not by any means. But in my grief, I had isolated myself, even from God.

I read on and it was the next verse that stopped me in my tracks.

I have no recollection what version of the Bible I was reading at the time, but I recall the next verse jumped off the page at me when I read, "I will be found by you," declares the Lord, "and I will restore that which I have taken from you."

My heart almost stopped beating. I was silent. I knew in my soul that God had another husband for me. I cried out to him, "Lord, please, anything but another husband." I listed afflictions I would rather receive in place of the demands of another marriage.

Thankfully, God didn't answer that prayer; he stayed his hand from any of the named afflictions. A couple of weeks later, the man God intended for me moved into my small circle of friends.

Two of my colleagues, a married couple named Vince and Carrie, thought that one of their friends would be a good match for me, and I for him. Knowing how I felt about relationships, they went about the introduction covertly. They invited me to join their Bible study group on one of their socials. They were going to see the animated Disney movie *The Lion King,* which was all the rage in 1994. Eager to see the movie, I agreed to join them.

We were just a small group of six: my married friends, another single woman, two single men, and me. After the movie, we went for coffee. I was not in a conversational mood. It had been a year since I'd been widowed and my depression was deepening. My friends were aware of this and did not force me into conversation. My lack of participation was clearly picked up by the others at the table and the conversation continued around me. I was also not particularly interested in either of the single men. I was sure they were nice enough, but I was not looking for a relationship or even new friends at this stage.

During the evening, one of the men excused himself from the table to go to the restroom. When he made his way back to our table, I happened to glance up at him as he weaved his way through the restaurant. I felt my body wake up. It tingled and went on full alert at his maleness. I couldn't help taking a closer look at him. What was it about this quiet, unassuming man that my body found desirable?

That night, on the way home with my friends, the car door was no sooner shut than Carrie started to tell me what a nice man Michiel Smit was. My body was already in agreement with her, so I listened as she told me about the good job he had, how respected he was by their Bible study group and their church community, and other credentials that essentially painted him as a good catch. I didn't say a word.

The next day was my infant nephew Jared's baptism. As we stood in the warm winter sun on the steps of Springs Catholic Church, I turned to Mom and said, "I think I was set up last night."

And set up I was.

But in the kindest, gentlest way.

Michiel and I "bumped into" each other again via the same friends, once, twice, and then the third time we had a date, of sorts. I was a school teacher and, as it was close to the end of the school year, I had a number of year-end social engagements to attend. I indicated to Carrie that I would attend the various school dances on my own as I didn't see the need to take a partner with me.

"Oh no, you can't do that," she replied. "We can ask Michiel Smit to go with you. He'll be happy to do it; he does it all the time when someone needs a date."

I later learned that was a stretch of the truth. Michiel was a quiet, reserved man who was on the shy side, particularly when it came to interacting with women. Yet, at the time, it gave me a sense of comfort that it would only be a "help-me-out" sort of date and not an actual date.

"I'll give him a call and ask him for you," Carrie added.

And she did. And he said yes. And we had a wonderful time.

A year later, I married that quiet, reserved man. And my friend was right, he was a good catch. In fact, I thought that he was too good for me, more than I deserved. He was everything I wasn't. He was a strong Christian who had waited faithfully and patiently for his wife. I had gone off the rails, moved in with my boyfriend, had a complicated marriage, and was shamed by my husband's suicide. He was emotionally stable, whereas, soon after we met, I started counselling for depression. He was financially solid. I was broke. He was Protestant. I was Catholic.

His family had some social standing, whereas mine did not. His family skeletons were hard to discern. Mine were very apparent.

What was he thinking?

He proposed six months after we met, and I accepted.

Michiel seemed so different from my first husband, and the circles we moved in now so far from my life in the country, that I could almost pretend that my first marriage never happened. Eighteen months after we married, we immigrated halfway around the world to Vancouver, Canada. I saw this as an opportunity for me to start my life anew and leave all of my hurt, embarrassment, and shame behind me.

However, while I lived a "normal" life in Canada, where no one knew my history of hurts, visits to South Africa meant spending time with my father. On those trips, rather than keep my distance from Dad, I would try to befriend him in some way, and in the process I would get hurt. I'd sit with him while he drank his beers after work or while we were together on holiday and make conversation. I was still looking for him to change, to be a caring dad, to love me the way I wanted him to. I was looking for him to not put himself and his drink first. It didn't happen.

On September 23, 2008, I realized I needed help. I needed to change my insane behavior. It was a warm and sunny South African afternoon, and Michiel's and my thirteenth wedding anniversary. Mom was having a family lunch to celebrate. While my brother, Clinton, barbequed, his wife Tracy, Michiel, and I sat around the swimming pool enjoying the sun and a refreshing drink. We sat with Dad who was habitually long into his drink of beers. Mom kept herself busy inside the cottage.

It was an innocuous moment, an innocuous request. Tracy asked my father to help with the barbeque. He exploded in anger. The venom spewed. It doesn't matter what he said. What matters is that he did it again. He spoiled yet another family gathering with his uncontrollable behavior, giving no thought to anyone but himself.

The tears welled up in me and I fled. That day, I knew I was at a crossroads.

These were not tears of anger or frustration. These were not heart-wrenching sobs. These were the long-buried tears of old emotion that

I could not stop. The tears ran. My father had broken my heart again.

First Mom came to console me, and we cried in each other's arms. Tracy came to check on us and she shook her head. "He does this all the time," she said. "Just ignore him. He hates that. Act as if he isn't there."

They both encouraged me to rejoin the family, but I wasn't ready to come back. I needed to be alone.

A short while later, Michiel found me in the backyard, tears running down my cheeks. "Brenda, come back," he coaxed me. "He didn't mean that."

I couldn't speak. Tears flowed. I shook my head—no. I couldn't go back and pretend everything was okay, not anymore.

"It's the drink talking," Michiel encouraged me again. "Come back and join us."

Eventually I did. And when I rejoined them, Dad tried to engage me with some benign comment, but I didn't respond. I was done with this game.

Later, he thanked me for washing the dishes.

I wanted to say, "Is that your apology?" Instead, all I mustered was, "You're welcome" and walked out of the cottage.

Back home, I shared my experience with a recovering alcoholic friend. We were helping to repaint our friend's apartment, and as John and I painted the door jamb to the bathroom, I told him my story.

"Should I attend Al-Anon?" I asked.

No. He recommended instead that I attend Celebrate Recovery, a Christian-based twenty-six-week recovery program being offered at our church. Based on the eight principles of the beatitudes, Celebrate Recovery is for anyone suffering from a hurt, a habit, or a hang-up. Or, like me, all three.

I took his advice and started the program.

At first, whenever I started to speak about my father, my feelings, or my experiences, I cried. It's a wonder I managed to say anything. Dad did not tolerate tears and so, in my adult life, I have had to learn to cry and be comfortable with tears and to understand that emotion, and sadness in particular, is okay. It is a real and acceptable feeling. The more I spoke about my family history and broke the secrecy around it, the easier it became for me to accept that history myself and to talk about it outside of the recovery group.

But the toughest lesson of all was realizing that my father would never be the father I wanted him to be. I clearly remember the day I was sharing in the group about something I wanted of my father and Lois McCann, the facilitator of our group and a recovering alcoholic and life-survivor herself, looked me in the eye and said to me, "He cannot give you what he doesn't have to give."

I was stunned and hurt by her words. I didn't want to hear them. Surely, that wasn't true. Surely, it wasn't an unrealistic expectation of mine that my dad be a good father to me; isn't that what all fathers should be? I still lived with the dream that somehow, at some time in the future, my father would shower affection on me and love me as his beautiful little girl, the apple of his eye. To accept Lois's words as true would mean death to that dream and death to my hope that, one day, my father and I could have a normal father-daughter relationship. It also meant death to my hope that, eventually, I could go out in public with my father and feel proud to be with him rather than embarrassed.

As hard as it was to hear those words, I knew that, once again, I had a choice. I could accept them and change my expectations of my father, or I could choose not to, in which case I would continue to perpetuate my need-filled behavior, behavior that was hurting me. I chose to accept the words as true. After all, I was there to change and one of the first steps to recovery is to admit that there is a problem and, subsequently, to step out of denial.

Another of Lois's sobering statements was, "And what is your part in this?" I would share about something difficult in my relationship with my Dad and that is what she would ask, "What is your part in this?"

What did she mean, what is my part in this? I'm not the one who is wrong here. I'm not the one drinking and hurting people and causing a ruckus. Are you crazy? What do you mean what is my part in this?

But there was no back chat or even opportunity for conversation in Celebrate Recovery. When it was your time to share, you did just that, you shared. Lois might give you feedback, or she might not, and then it was the next person's turn to share. This was about doing your homework, sharing, and listening to what surfaced in your heart and to what the Holy Spirit revealed to you. This was not about fixing anyone else. If there was any input at all, whether it be supportive or challenging, it came from Lois only.

Through Celebrate Recovery I learned what it was to be an enabler and to be co-dependent in a dysfunctional relationship. That helped me to identify, now that I was an adult, what indeed was my part and my responsibility in my difficult relationship with my father.

I came to realize, and accept, that my father did not love me the way I wanted him to—and that he probably never would. It hurt deeply. I needed to feel that hurt, grieve it, mourn it, and let it go. I also needed to learn new ways of interacting with my father, for my sake. I stopped looking to my father for the things he could not give me: acceptance, affection, and acknowledgement. I recognized him as a sad, angry man who had lost his life to resentments and, in burying his own hurts, had lost himself in drink.

Acknowledging this gave me a new way of dealing with my father. Although the triggers were still there, I knew to limit the amount of time I spent in his company when he was drinking. As I was no longer looking for things from him that he couldn't give me, the time I did spend with him was free of those expectations. The hurts were not fully healed and the shame was still very real, but they didn't have the same hold over me. I had also named the enemy.

My father was not just a heavy drinker. He was not just someone who liked his beers. He was an alcoholic. And I came to accept that. Until he decided that he'd had enough, there was nothing I could do to rescue him. But I could pray for him. That was the only weapon I had to fight for the soul of my father. That, and my own desire for God to transform me so that I could live from my broken, often-assaulted heart.

CHAPTER THIRTEEN

God continued to change my perspective in my relationship with my father from the book *Jesus Today* by Albert Nolan. I was challenged by Nolan's perspective on loving others, an approach I had not considered before.

"Before we can come to love other people as they are, we need to learn to love ourselves as we are—unconditionally. We will not be able to overcome our selfishness until we resolve our inner conflicts and learn to live at peace with ourselves. Most of us are divided against ourselves. We need to become whole. Jesus was at peace with himself."[25]

Part of coming to love myself involved resolving the inner conflict of shame I felt about my father and our family dynamics. I needed to go even deeper and further than I had thus far with Celebrate Recovery. Celebrate Recovery had helped me to expose and discuss my feelings about my father. It had given me understanding about some of the dynamics of my family. It had helped me to establish boundaries with myself in relation to my father. It had revealed to me the unrealistic expectations I had of him. It had given me a forum to work through my hurt, my guilt, and my shame.

Now, God wanted to do an even deeper healing work in me. He wanted me to experience the deep love he has for humankind by stirring in me his love for my father, a love that is non-judgmental and fully compassionate, a love that meets us exactly where we are at.

However, as Albert Nolan advised, I needed to start with myself. I needed to learn to accept my shame. Although I was a new creation in Christ, a born-again Christian to use the evangelical term, I still needed to accept my family and my family history. God was not going to wipe the slate clean and make us a perfect family; rather, it was time for me to accept my shame. As Nolan explains, acceptance is not the same as resignation, rather, "... accepting my shadow side means I embrace it and love it as part of who I am. Resignation perpetuates the inner conflict. Loving acceptance enables me to begin to live at peace with myself. In the final analysis, it is a matter of humility, of embracing the whole truth about myself,"[26] which included the whole truth of my family. The truth I so desperately wanted to rewrite.

I had already made steps in that direction by revealing the secret that I was the daughter of an alcoholic, and sharing how it had impacted my life so far. However, I still felt deeply embarrassed about my father and his circumstances. And those circumstances were not getting any better. In fact, they were growing progressively worse. How I longed for redemption in my family and for my father. How I longed for a happy ending and success story that would see my father, the drinker, repent and become an upstanding citizen who would be a living testimony to the redemptive work of Jesus Christ in his life. How I longed to see a miracle in his life that only God could bring about. A miracle that would include a close and healthy relationship with his daughter. But the reports I was getting from South Africa were far from that. He was becoming increasingly steeped in his alcoholism, and the weekends, when he was off work, were the worst. He drank all the time and became confrontational and hurtful.

Dad needed to be admitted to a treatment center. But who was going to be bold enough to intervene and make it happen? I wasn't there, and could I do it even if I was? Two of my brothers didn't think that it would make any difference, so why try? Wouldn't it be better to just wait it out? From Dad there was no indication whatsoever that he was interested in getting better or changing his trajectory of self-destruction. I got a book out of the library on alcoholism. Given the explanation of alcoholism and a description that depicted Dad's current circumstances, I realized that my father was in the final stages of the disease.

Dad had been a committed drinker since he was a teen. It started the way it does for many alcoholics; he was just one of the boys out to have some fun. On Friday nights after work, or on the weekend after a game of water polo, he would meet his friends at the pub for drinks. Over the years, drinking became an integral part of Dad's life, his go-to method of coping with life's difficulties.

After Mom's death, Dad's drinking, which until then had been moderated by her presence, became chronic. He switched from beer to vodka, and once he started drinking he was unable to stop. A year after Mom's death, Mark took a month's absence from his community in order to spend time with Dad. He also visited and stayed over as often as he could to keep Dad company and to take some of the pressure off Clinton and Tracy. While Mark was there, Dad would ease up on his drinking and eat more. However, Dad's housekeeper observed that the minute Mark left, sometimes while his car was still backing out the driveway, Dad would go hard at it again. In October 2015, Dad stopped working and we held our collective breaths. At least with his job, his drinking was interrupted by his need to go to work. But now that he had nothing to do and no reason to go anywhere, the excessive drinking of the weekends became an everyday event.

During this time of worry and concern and praying for Dad, God was teaching me how to love freely like he does, with the starting point being me, not my father.

Increasingly, I accepted that Dad, as an alcoholic, was not going to change. I found that my acceptance first began in my head, when I realized that there was a problem. Then it moved to my mouth as I started to talk about it. Acceptance's next destination was my heart, where I mourned and grieved my losses. Once I did that, my heart and my head started to align and peace began to germinate. The final and transformative destination was my soul, where acceptance hit at the core of my being. When I lovingly received and embraced my dysfunctional relationship with my father in the fiber of my being, and welcomed it as an integral part of who I am, my shame and anger begin to dissipate. In their place, God let compassion and peace flourish. It was in accepting my shame that God replaced it. I had wanted God to eradicate my shame and save me from the process of facing it and accepting it. Once again, God's starting point was different from mine. It was only in accepting my shame that I met with the deep peace of God and I could start to experience compassion for my father and for the brokenness in mankind.

None of this was achieved with a flick of a switch. It came from abiding with him. It came from being still and knowing that God is God. It came from trusting, come what may. It came from a deep sense from within that I wanted a deeper relationship with God, one of greater trust and transformation. And it came from listening and doing what I believed God was telling me to do. As tempting as it was, I chose not to give bitterness, cynicism, and anger a foothold.

When I first accepted myself and my faults, and how much I was still in need of Jesus' ongoing transformation in my life, I could more easily embrace my father and his faults, and love him as he was.

It was at this cross-section that my life in Jesus deepened. He started to free me from the pursuit of the perfect life and the perfect family. I was able to let go of any need I had for social standing and social acceptance. I could also more easily release any desire for material possessions to showcase my worth and value to myself and to the watching world. He loosened my grip on my comforters: food, alcohol, work, pride, perfectionism, the need to be right. All false comforters that filled my angst that I was not good enough just as I was. False comforters are stepping stones to addictions, and addictions, I've learned, are symptoms of our deep hurts, brokenness, and angst.

In learning to love my father as he was, and by looking to Jesus to fill the emotional holes in my life, I further freed my father from any expectation to meet my needs. As Nolan would say, I removed the burden I had put on his shoulders and unleashed the chain with which I had tied him—and myself—down.

However, as Nolan enlightened me, this freedom from expectation is not an end in itself but rather "it is a means to something greater, namely, doing the will of God. I am not called to be perfectly free, I am called to do God's will."[27]

For me, my freedom came as I accepted that my father could not, nor would he ever, love me the way I wanted him to. My freedom came when

I accepted and embraced the truth that my father was an alcoholic. My freedom came when I stopped covering for him and when I stopped trying to make my family something that it wasn't. My freedom came when I acknowledged that my family and I were of no consequence in this "pursuit of status" world. I wanted to be someone, but I was no one. I wanted my family to be somebodies, but they were nobodies. My freedom came when I stopped looking up the ladder and looked, instead, long and hard at where I had come from. My freedom came, not when I stopped climbing the ladder, but when I started to go back down. My freedom came when I said, "Not my will, but your will be done, whatever that may be."

I reached that place in February 2016 when, based on a passage from *Jesus Today*, I noted this in my journal:

I am God's handiwork, a significantly small but unique part of God's great ongoing work of art. And, when I allow God to work in and through me, I become a co-artist and a co-creator in the future. When I am radically free or on the way to radical freedom, divine energy can flow through me unhindered. This divine energy, the Holy Spirit, is infinitely powerful, creative, and healing... I choose to give up doing my own thing and I choose to begin to participate in the only work that is effective and real: God's work.[28]

Concern and compassion for Dad increased as I walked with God and took becoming more like Jesus seriously. I had to again accept that this wasn't about doing things my way according to my will. It was about trust and hope in God. It was about waiting for his timing, and resting in him, knowing that his way could look very different from my way. It was about being comfortable with that because I trusted God.

I did still worry about Dad, though. It was hard not to feel anxious about his drinking, about what he was doing to himself, and about the strain it was putting on everyone, particularly Clinton and his family. Again, God spoke into my concern.

On February 16, 2016, on what would have been my parents' fifty-third wedding anniversary, I was unpacking the dishwasher and putting the clean dishes into the kitchen cupboard, thinking about my father and worrying about his situation as I worked. As I reached up to put glasses into the cupboard I *heard* a whisper, "Don't worry."

The next morning in my journal, again loosely based on an excerpt from *Jesus Today*, I responded with these words:

In becoming more spiritually mature, I realize that it is imperative that I do this—trust you and don't worry. It doesn't mean that I become inactive. I still move forward and do things—enquire, look, research—all in the spirit of trusting you and not worrying. I also need to listen for your direction. It's a real lesson in reliance. As you say Jesus, "who of you by worrying can add one day (or hour or minute) to your life?" In fact, I take away from it. I become radically free when I follow Jesus' example and put all my trust and hope in God.

I received God's guidance and endeavored to not worry. But it was a daily, even hourly exercise to place my concern with God and leave it there.

On February 24, 2016, I wrote in my journal:

It is a fine line between worry and concern. Worry: it's about negative experiences and outcomes that I can't control. Concern: it's about what my father is intentionally putting himself through, this slow suicide, the pressure and anxiety it puts on the family, his standing with you. I am left with prayer and powerlessness. I am powerless to do anything except pray. And to be honest, I feel that so often prayer is ineffective. Why do I pray? You are the almighty, autonomous God who is unfair and will do what you want anyway. Who am I to change your mind? How long have I been praying for my dad? What has changed? He is more calcified in his stubbornness. He's become a rampant alcoholic who has isolated himself by driving everyone away. He's rude and cantankerous, selfish and self-centered. So where is the change for good as a result of prayer in any of that?

I poured out my heart to God in my journal:

At night my soul cries out and prays for him, and what has that helped? Will my father be defiant and rebellious to his dying day, which is not too far now? Is Michiel right? Did you know this and it was all about changing me and my heart towards him? You don't want a single person to be lost—Lord save him. Let him cry out to you. Let his soul call to you because I know that you will hear him. I know that you are closer to him than his breath, yet still, that doesn't mean that you will save him if he doesn't want to be saved. He's punishing himself—it's not about penance, it's about forgiveness—if only he would turn to you.

Lord, I exhort you that you yourself search for Ken James, this lost and injured sheep. Look after him. Rescue him from the wilderness he has driven himself into in his days of darkness. Bring him out of that darkness and gather him to yourself. Bring him into the everlasting kingdom. He doesn't deserve it—and nor do I. Let him turn and accept your gracious gift of forgiveness and redemption through Jesus. Tend your sheep—even the wayward, wild, and defiant ones. Lord, you say that you will search for the lost and bring back the strays. I charge you, Lord, be true to your word. Bind up the broken and strengthen the weak as you say you will. Lord, my God, I plead on behalf of my father—be true to who you are and rescue this lost, battered, and defiant sheep. Take him home safe in your arms.

Two days later, I wrote:

I put my father in your care. Love him deeply for me. Life is hard and, at times, I get tired of living.

And a few days after that entry, on March 3, I wrote:

A feeling of bonheur and at the same time deep concern for
Dad. I awake thinking of him. I pray for him in my sleep.

During this time of prayer and concern for Dad, a question stirred
deep within me: should I go see Dad? I had learned my lesson from the
experience with Mom. I had left going to see her too late. I did not want
to leave reaching out to Dad too late.

After Mom's death I had deep regrets, not only that I had emigrated,
but also that I had emigrated so far away. If it was just one flight, I could
have been there overnight, but from the West Coast of Canada it was
triple that travel time. I also deeply regretted that I hadn't been there to
help Mom, to accompany her on her trips to the hospital, to encourage
her and to care for her, to shower my love on her. I didn't want to have
similar regrets with Dad. I grappled with worry and concern about him
and his circumstances.

My concern for Dad increased with Mark's planned trip to visit
our brother, Grant, in Australia for a month. I knew that Mark was
Dad's closest companion, and even though Mark could only see Dad
periodically, Dad enjoyed his company whenever my brother could stay
over. In mid-March, Mark moved from Pietermaritzburg to Springs
to take up the position of parish priest of Kwa-Thema, a township of
Springs, in order to live closer to Dad and to offer support to Clinton
and Tracy. Mark's absence from the end of March to the end of April
would put more pressure on Clinton and Tracy, as Dad's behavior and
drinking worsened when he was alone. I felt increasingly that I should
go and spend time with him. Michiel and I already had a trip to South
Africa planned for the end of September that year, but given the news
that Dad was often lying in bed, debilitated by pain from his leg, crippled
from the time he had fallen off a ladder, I thought I should go and see
him sooner rather than later. I also needed to see the situation with my
own eyes rather than rely on reports from my siblings.

At the end of March, Michiel and I called Dad to let him know that
I was going to come and visit him for two weeks. I braced myself for the

usual nonchalant reply. Perhaps he would say, "Don't worry about me, Miss Ann. I'm fine." Or, "Don't waste your money on a ticket. Spend your money on something else. Go buy linens." Which is what he had said to me when I first told him that I was going to come out and see Mom when she was ill. But instead he said, "That's a good idea, especially now that Mark is away."

Mark had been in Australia just a few days when I called to let him know that I would be going out to spend time with Dad. Mark was greatly relieved at the news.

"Now I can relax and enjoy my holiday," he said.

I knew that my visiting Dad would be a gift to Mark. It was going to be good for me too and, hopefully, a blessing for Dad. It was a promising start that he was open to my visit.

CHAPTER FOURTEEN

The morning I walked into Dad's cottage, after arriving late the night before, he was sitting on the couch watching TV.

"Morning, Dad," I said.

"I thought you changed your mind and you weren't coming," he replied.

"No. I said I was coming." I bent down and gave him a kiss.

"Do you want a cup of tea?"

No, he didn't. I put the kettle on and made a cup for myself. Dad, I discovered, no longer drank tea, he only drank vodka and ginger-ale and filled his glass at a 1:1 ratio.

I had already decided that I didn't want to dig up old hurts with him. I just wanted to be there with him, to love and accept him as he was, to show him unconditional love without any expectation that he be different from who he was, or what he was, or where he was at this time of his life. My primary relationship was with God, not anyone else. My identity was in Christ, not in my father. My guidance was from the Holy Spirit, not my fickle emotions. My approach towards Dad was going to be one of accepting him as he was without voicing, in any way, that he should change. God had changed me; my heart was compassionate towards my father. For years his drinking had been a wedge between us. Now I was going to spend time with him, when he was at his drinking worst, and just be there with him.

When my brother, Clinton, had picked me up from the airport he warned me that I might be shocked to see Dad as he was swollen and puffy with poor coloring. For sure, Dad didn't look good, but he didn't look as bad as I had imagined he would. What I did notice, though, was how unkempt he was. Dad believed in shaving every day, he'd never been one for stubble, but now it was strong on his chin and sides of his face. His sweatpants were comfortable, given his crippled leg, but they were tired with holes and marks on them. His nails were long and jagged as though he had started to cut some of them, had struggled to do it, and then given up. I had expected to see my father unwell; I hadn't expected to see him untidy and disheveled.

I didn't comment on any of it. I didn't offer to cut his fingernails. I didn't suggest that he shave or put on other clothes. I didn't even bring it to his attention when the mucous ran from his nose as his body struggled to deal with the toxicity in his system. My father was not a pretty picture. But God kept my tongue still and my eyes compassionate.

I remembered a counselor once advising that, when dealing with someone who is depressed, we can feel that we are helping them by doing things for them or encouraging them to do things for themselves. But often the first step is to just sit and be with them. Be blind to the things that they aren't doing and should do. Just sit with them and share their pain. If you arrive, she suggested, and their home is a mess, the windows cloudy with grime, don't start cleaning. Don't wash the window and say, "Look outside and see what a beautiful day it is." Don't point to the activities outside the window and say, "You should get outside and take a walk." Sit with them in their pain.

As slovenly as Dad's appearance was, his cottage was immaculate. His housekeeper, Johanna Thusi, cleaned his cottage every week day. Everything was in its place and Dad liked it that way. When Mom was alive the cottage was tidy, but now it was pristine. However, Mom's joy, her garden, was sadly neglected. Her potato tree was overgrown and shooting wildly from its base. The creeper she had been training on a trellis was stretching out of control in all directions, twining its tendrils around the nearby perennial geraniums and rose bushes. The dead, leafless stalks of a hydrangea that had not survived the previous winter stood sentry-like near the back door. Weeds shot up all over the garden and ground cover grew unchecked into the grass. What was already a small patch of grass had been made smaller still as the neighbor's hedges grew over the wall, crowded out the light, and caused the grass to die and the ground to become a dust bowl. Dirt and dry leaves collected along the walkway to the cottage, in the dry birdbath, and on the small patio. It was hard for me to see Mom's garden so neglected and Dad so disheveled.

After my cup of tea, I looked in Dad's fridge and asked if he wanted eggs and bacon for breakfast. Yes, he did. I scrambled eggs and fried back bacon. I sliced bread and made toast. I set the table and we sat down to eat together. Dad devoured the scrambled eggs, but struggled with the bacon and ended up leaving it on the plate with the toast. After that, bacon wasn't on the breakfast menu. It was too difficult for Dad to chew and, I realized later, too hard for his stomach to digest.

For lunch, I offered to make him chips, a favorite of his. Johanna, who was doing his housework, gave me a hug when she heard me make the offer.

"I love you," she said.

"Why?" I asked.

"Because the old man loves chips," she answered.

I'm not a great shake chip-maker, but my first batch wasn't too bad and Dad and I ate chips for lunch. On day two, I bought Dad a steak pie for lunch. He received it gladly and I left him to eat it while I went outside. When I returned, the pie was finished and the plate empty except for crumbs. I was pleased. I had been hoping that Dad would eat more. I tried not to kid myself; Dad could likely put up a good front for a day or two, but not for the full two weeks of my trip. This would give me a good picture of the reality of his situation.

On my first day, he finished his bottle of vodka and didn't have a replacement. He couldn't go out and buy another because one of his grandsons was using his car. But he also didn't call my brother or his wife to ask that they stop by the liquor store and get him another bottle, which is what he would normally do. Instead, he drank the rest of his ginger-ale neat. By the late afternoon, his thirst was unquenchable and he asked me to bring the bottle of milk from the fridge. His hands shook uncontrollably when he reached out to take it from me. Dad drank two liters of milk, clearly trying to slake his thirst. He wasn't interested in dinner. How would he survive the night, I wondered.

That evening as Clinton, Tracy, and I talked casually in their kitchen, leaning against the counter and sipping our wine, I glanced up and across the courtyard. Dad stood at the window of his kitchen, watching us. As much as we were illuminated by a bright light, Dad's kitchen was in darkness. However, his outline was distinguishable because of the soft light of the lamp that stood next to the couch in his living room.

Seeing Dad in his window watching us, I was struck by this thought: *Dad, the outsider looking in.* A second thought followed quickly after: *I think that's who he has been all his life.*

My heart softened and ached for him.

The next morning, Dad's shakes were less obvious and, after our breakfast, he headed out to take his car to be looked at by his mechanic and to run some errands. I offered to go with him, but he said he was fine on his own. I was relieved; I didn't really want to drive with him. He returned an hour and a bit later with a story about his trip to the post office and a fresh supply of vodka.

Dad and I slipped into a routine. He liked to take an early bath and head for bed around six. I would then return to the main house for the evening. In the morning I would go over to his cottage around nine, or once he opened his back door, whichever was later. I wanted to be company for Dad, but I didn't want to be in his face. We had never spent time together like this before. It was new ground for both of us.

After breakfast, I would wash the dishes instead of leaving them for Johanna. With the housework at the main house too, she had enough to do. Besides which, it gave me something to do while in Dad's company. In the morning Dad liked to sit on the kitchen stool with his back against the wall, right next to the back door. It was there that the sunshine came through the kitchen window and fell on the counter and the stool. He'd smoke his cigarettes and drink the vodka that had replaced his morning cup of tea. I never commented on it except to ask one day why he had switched from beer to vodka.

"Because the beer wasn't agreeing with my stomach," he said.

I didn't call him on his cover-up. There were other cover-ups too, and I didn't call him on any of those either. Perhaps I should have, but I didn't.

One day, I tried my hand at a beef bourguignon recipe, one that was too strong on red wine. I prepped and chopped and put all the ingredients in Mom's slow cooker. Again, cooking in Mom's kitchen meant that I could be in Dad's company but not in his space. While I was busy, Dad would watch TV or sit in his corner drinking, or go and lie down because his leg pained him so. When the beef bourguignon was ready, I ladled some into a cup to taste it. Dad liked the look of it and asked to sample it too. He took a sip and his face reacted as the richness of the sauce hit the raw lining of his vodka-scorched stomach. Discouraged, I threw what was left of the sample back into the pot.

The next morning I washed the dishes, including Mom's slow cooker. I carefully wiped the outside, giving it a good onceover. I wiped the electrical cord. I washed the lid and the ceramic pot and dried them. All done, I turned to place the slow cooker on the dining room table and looked up. Dad had been watching my every move from his spot in the living room. His face exuded softness.

"It's so clean; it's as good as new," he said.

"Yes, Michiel taught me to clean like that," I replied.

"That's good. That's how it should be."

I realized again how neat and clean Dad liked things to be. If I left the sliding cupboard door above the kitchen sink open, he asked me to close it. While his body and life fell apart, his home was orderly and spotless. Admittedly, Dad didn't actually do much to disturb things in his cottage. He moved from his bed, to the couch, to the fridge, to his drinking spot, to the bathroom, and back again. And there was always Johanna, his faithful housekeeper, to clean his cottage for him.

One morning, I thanked Johanna for the great care she took of my father. Some of the cleaning she had to do was not pretty, to say the least. It was self-less care, done in a spirit of Christ-filled servitude.

"I know it isn't always easy," I said to Johanna. "The old man can be difficult. Yet, you do it with such a loving spirit."

"I do it for your mother," Johanna replied. "Your mother was very good to me. And I promised her that I would take care of the old man."

I hugged Johanna. She was being true to her promise to my mother. Even after her death, Dad was benefitting from Mom's legacy of extending kindness, compassion, and love to others.

Johanna, I realized, had been a confidant and friend to my mother during her illness. After Mom died, I approached Johanna as she stood among piles of sorted clothes and filled the washing machine. I asked how she was doing with the news of my mother's death. Johanna spoke of my mother, of their relationship, and of her love for Mom. She told me how my mother would tell her, "I love all my children, Johanna, and you are one of my children."

She also recounted how she would hear Mom put on a brave voice while talking to me when I called, giving the impression that things weren't as serious as they actually were. When she hung up from our call on one of those days, Johanna said to her, "Madam, why do you tell your daughter that everything is okay when you are sick? You must tell her that you are sick."

My mother replied, "I don't want her to see me this way."

And then Johanna wrapped Mom in her arms as my mother cried.

Soon after I arrived, I noticed that my presence gave Dad some comfort. While I was watching TV with him within the first few days of my visit, Dad turned and said to me, "I don't bother to shave anymore."

"Well, you are not going anywhere," I replied.

"That's what I say." He seemed surprised and pleased at my response. His countenance actually brightened a little and he sat up a touch straighter.

The next morning when I walked into the cottage, he was at his bathroom mirror, shaving. Later that day, while we again watched TV together, I said, "You look better having shaved. It looks good."

Dad shaved more regularly after that, but not consistently.

To pass the time, I thought I would spend some of it writing. The weather in early April was still lovely and warm. So, one afternoon, I set up a small table on the veranda outside the cottage's back door, threw a tablecloth over it, placed my laptop on it, pulled up my chair, and typed away at a story. I finished, packed up, and moved the table to the side, out the way of the walkway and closer to the back door.

I was in the bathroom of my brother's house, washing my hands, when I heard a mighty crash. I dried my hands quickly, rushed through the kitchen, out the back door, across the little courtyard, and opened the gate to Dad's garden. He had gotten tangled up with my writing table and was struggling to get up.

"I fell out of my slipper," he said as I helped him to his feet. Indeed the slipper lay separated from my father's foot, but I'm sure it was more the unsteadiness of his legs and feet that caused him to fall.

I looked him up and down. "Are you bleeding or hurt?"

There was only evidence of a small cut on his hand. Dad wouldn't own up to any other bruising or pain. It was part of the cover-up, but Dad was not a whiner; when he suffered, he did so in silence. I think Dad saw his pain as his penance. Mom had not died an easy death, so why should he be spared suffering?

The first two days I was with him, Dad released deep sighs. It was something I had noticed him doing in the days following Mom's death, deep sighs for no apparent reason. Once I returned to Canada, I caught myself also emitting deep sighs for no particular reason. I realized later that it was part of the process of coming to accept the reality of Mom's death. Now, twenty-one months later, Dad was again sighing long, deep sighs. At first I thought it was because he was stuck in his grief, but he stopped after a few days. He resumed the sighing on the last day of my visit, although this time it was slightly different. The sighs were more shallow and were followed by Dad saying, "Ja, Miss Ann," using his nickname for me, as though he was acknowledging something. It clearly wasn't an invitation for me to engage him.

I believe Dad's initial sighing was because he was adjusting to my presence and I was a reminder to him of my mother. On the last day, I believe it was because he was adjusting to the fact that he was going to be left alone again. As my departure date drew closer, Dad asked me when Mark was expected back from Australia. Mark was due to return nine days after I left.

CHAPTER FIFTEEN

"Miss Ann, can you come and help me with my shirt?" Dad called to me from the bathroom.

I hesitated.

"I'm decent," he called again.

I put down the dish towel and opened the door to the bathroom. Dad was struggling with the last two buttons. He was also struggling to stand. I unbuttoned the shirt and helped him out of it. I pulled the bathroom door closed behind me and continued with washing the dishes while Dad took his nightly bath. I was finishing up when I heard an almighty crack, like a gun shot. I dropped the dish cloth and opened the door to the bathroom. I could just see the back of Dad's head and the side of his face. He appeared to be in excruciating pain from knocking his head on the tub.

"Hold on, Dad," I cried. "I'm going to call Clinton."

I ran across to the main house to get my brother. Clinton came back with me, leaving his cigarette burning on the edge of the outdoor table.

"What's up, Dad?" he asked as he walked into the bathroom. He helped Dad out of the bath and left him to dry and dress himself. We stood outside the back door. Clinton smoked as he shared how tired he and his family felt dealing with Dad and his drinking. I listened.

The next morning, when I walked into the cottage, Dad was again sitting on the couch watching a rerun on TV. "How's your head, Dad?"

"It's fine," he said with chagrin. "I just knocked it."

"Yes, and it was some knock too."

I decided not to pursue it any further. The time for our discussions usually happened later in the day, when Dad was in his sunny corner of the kitchen propped on his stool, back against the wall, drinking his glass of half-vodka, half-ginger-ale while I washed the dishes.

"Dad," I said as I dried a dish, "you shouldn't take a bath unless someone is here to help you. You put in a fair bit of water and one day you could slip, knock your head, and drown in the bath."

Dad didn't reply. But after that, for the most part, he took his baths while I was still there so I could either help him or call my brother to help. Clinton had installed a grip in the bath to assist him, but Dad didn't always have enough strength to pull himself up. And when he did, he had to try to balance himself with two unsteady legs, one of them crippled.

There were times I helped Dad to bed, before his bath, because he'd had too much to drink. Each time he was so appreciative of my efforts. I was touched by the genuineness in his "thank you" when I pulled the covers over him. Not that Dad looked at all comfortable in bed. His leg caused him untold pain and he couldn't lie down easily.

There were times, when he thought I wasn't looking, that Dad would rub his leg and I could see the pain in his unguarded face.

"Dad, why don't you take a painkiller?" I asked one day.

"Because I am not a pill popper," he replied.

"But taking a painkiller to relieve genuine pain doesn't mean that you are a pill popper. It is a smart thing to do to give yourself relief."

Dad kept his pills on top of the wooden box where Mom had stored her flour. He refused to take his painkillers or his blood pressure medication or any of the other medications he had there.

"Your painkillers do say you need to be careful if you consume vast quantities of alcohol," I said as I read the insert, "so there is a risk involved, but which is the worse of two evils?"

Again Dad didn't say anything, but that night, when the pain was severe and he couldn't sleep for it or the confusion that the vodka caused in his system, he did take a couple of painkillers.

In an attempt to help him eat, I tried my hand at making Mom's beef vegetable soup, the one he liked so much. He was happy for the soup, but didn't eat any of the vegetables or meat. He left them at the bottom of his mug and threw them out. I blended some of the soup for him to help his stomach with digesting the vegetables. Dad ate less and less while I was there. His valiant attempts to eat grew fewer and fewer.

In the second week of my visit, I again bought him a steak pie for lunch. The meat was tender and it was one Dad liked. He nibbled at it. I stepped outside for a bit, came back in, and Dad's empty plate was next to the sink. He was sitting on the couch watching TV. I knew that there was absolutely no way he had eaten it that fast. I checked the garbage can, and there lay his pie in its final resting place. I left it there.

I had heard from Tracy that she often found the supper she had prepared for Dad in his garbage can, thrown out. We put it down to his being ungrateful about her cooking. Dad had been spoilt by Mom. She cooked all his favorite dishes and none of the ones he didn't like, such as chicken and pasta, go-to staples for Tracy, a working mother on a tight budget. Perhaps he initially did throw the suppers away because he was ungrateful, but I was certain that, by now, it was because he couldn't eat them, not because he didn't want to eat them.

As much as he couldn't eat food, Dad spoke about food, especially the memories they evoked for him. I bought some avocados and Dad watched them like a hawk, asking when they would be ripe. Unfortunately, they never did ripen. They were big, handsome avocados but, even though we put them on the ledge in the sun, they just never ripened.

Dad mentioned that he would love a piece of roast lamb. So I bought a leg of lamb and roasted it in the oven. We ate it for Sunday lunch at the main house. Dad came over to join us. He was pretty plastered, but still able to walk and hold himself up. I dished out the food and he asked me to cut his meat for him. He tried a couple of mouthfuls, but just couldn't do it. He got up, excused himself, and left the rest of us at the dinner table.

"Clinton, do you think your Dad needs help getting back?" Tracy asked.

"We'll hear soon enough," Clinton replied.

For all his gruffness, Dad had a sensitive side. He was hurt by the comment of a visiting guest of my brother's who had not seen Dad in a while and was shocked at his deterioration.

"So-and-so says that I look untidy." I could hear the hurt in Dad's voice. "I bathe every day. My clothes are clean."

"Perhaps it's because you haven't shaved. And your clothes look tired and have holes in them." I spoke as honestly and gently as I could. I didn't mention that his face showed the wear of his choices and his heartache.

The next morning, I noticed that Dad had chosen a different jersey and sweatpants, still comfortable for him with his crippled leg, but less worn and washed out. He had shaved again.

"Look here." Dad called to me after I had switched the kettle on to make tea. He showed me the deep bruises and marks on his arms from his crutches. "The crutches cut into me. I try to soften them with my jerseys, but they still do it."

His forearms were black and blue where they connected with the hard plastic of the crutch that encircled the arm. I started to make a suggestion of what else we could try.

"No, it's fine," Dad said. "Just leave it."

And so I did.

I spoke to Dad about his drinking a handful of times, and always in a matter-of-fact way.

One of the times occurred when we were in our usual routine, Dad at the kitchen counter drinking, me washing dishes or chopping vegetables. He looked across at the main house and, seeing my brother and his wife, commented, "They watch too much TV."

I came, stood next to Dad, and looked out of the window too.

"They should get on with their lives and not watch so much TV," he added.

"Well, Dad," I said, "your addiction is alcohol and their addiction is TV."

I walked back to the sink and picked up the next dish to dry.

Another opportunity arose when Dad was recounting a story to me. In his loneliness Dad had, in the past, gone over in the evening to visit at the main house. He would watch TV with my brother and his family and try to make conversation. "But no one talks to me," Dad told me.

I lifted my shoulders in a shrug and said in reply, "If you are going over when you've been drinking then no one is going to talk to you." I let that sink in before I added, "Besides which, they're not big conversationalists. And they're watching TV. That isn't always the best time to talk."

Another time I mentioned his drinking was after Dad had told me about a lady interest he had. It wasn't news to me as I had heard about it from my sister-in-law. I didn't know much about it as I hadn't pursued the topic when Tracy mentioned it. I wasn't particularly interested one way or the other.

"She actually pursued me," Dad said between sips. "She wanted to get involved."

I had to wonder at the sanity of any woman who wanted to get involved with my father, but I also knew that Dad had a very charming side and she would have known him before his drinking had gotten to this stage.

"So," I asked, "did you like her?"

Dad indicated that he did.

"Then, why didn't you?"

"She was too young," Dad said. "And besides, how would you feel if I married again?"

I still thought this woman needed her head read, but I answered honestly, "I would be okay with it. You're very lonely and I think it would be good for you. Provided she doesn't drink, because you do enough of that already."

Dad left the comment unanswered.

"What's stopping you now?"

"She moved away. But I'm not interested. I had a wife for fifty-one years."

Dad often referred to Mom, not as my mother, but as his wife of fifty-one years. Mom's death and Dad's subsequent regret had caused him to tap into that reservoir of deep love he had for her. I recognized it in me too. I loved Mom and I knew that I loved her. But her death revealed to me the depth of my love for her. When she was always just on the other end of the line, or waiting across the ocean for my next visit, ready to be embraced by me, my love for her was known but not experienced in every fiber of my being. Mom would always be there, why wouldn't she be? But when she was stolen from me and all my dreams for us with her, I felt the depth of my love for her within me.

And I believe that it was this love that Dad experienced now. When Mom was alive he could, at times, be cold and callous towards her. Certainly not mindful of her needs and certainly not always considerate. Sadly, Mom was more loved in her absence than in her presence. It took her death to change Dad.

In one of our discussions, I broached the topic of death and asked Dad how long he thought he might have to live.

He looked surprised and replied, "Ten years, two years. I don't know."

"Six months?" I asked.

"My Uncle Reggie drank a bottle of brandy a day and lived to eighty-one," he replied.

With that comparison in his mind, Dad thought that he could live another ten years.

"You could also die from cirrhosis of the liver. That's a difficult and painful way to die."

"Your Mom didn't die an easy death," he replied.

"No, she didn't." I dropped my gaze as the ache of missing my mother filled me. I pushed the memory of her death from my mind and reached for the next potato to peel.

I also broached the topic of Dad moving into a retirement home. Actually, he mentioned it first. He was telling me about some of his peers, including the previous principal at my primary school who was in a local old age home.

"Why don't you move into a retirement home?" I glanced up at Dad as I removed faded blooms from the flowers I had picked out of the garden.

Dad shook his head.

"You would have company and not be so lonely," I encouraged him.

"No," Dad replied, "I'm staying right here. I don't want to go anywhere. Brian, my brother, offered for me to go down and live in Cape Town near them and they would take care of me. But I'm staying here. I'm not going anywhere."

And he didn't want to go anywhere, not even out for a drive. When I was growing up, that was something he liked to do on a Sunday afternoon. All the shops would be closed and there were no activities going on in our little town on that day of rest. Dad would say, "Let's go out for a Sunday drive." Mom and I were always game. Dad would drive somewhere, anywhere, just there and back to see how far it was. Mom would knit and I would look out the window at the passing scenery. We wouldn't talk. We would just be.

"Do you want to go out for a drive?" I asked Dad one morning as I stirred my cup of tea.

"No," he replied. "I just want to stay here." And so we stayed home.

Dad's primary source of company and entertainment was the TV. He switched it on when he got up in the morning and switched it off when he went to bed at night. Even when he wasn't watching it, it droned from its corner of the living room, an impersonal companion.

"There's nothing on TV," Dad complained to me one day. "Just reruns of reruns. Your mother would say switch the TV off."

"And I would say, find another channel. You only watch two of them." I didn't mind watching BBC Earth with Dad. But I wasn't interested in his other channel, real-life murders.

"I can't understand," he would say, "how people can treat each other like this. How can they kill like this?"

And I can't understand why on earth you would watch it. But I let it go; I didn't say a word about his choice of shows. The next morning when I walked into the cottage, Dad was watching TV and his first words to me were, "I looked for some other stations to watch, but there aren't any."

I said nothing and put the kettle on.

Dad's biggest concern was money. He spoke incessantly about it, how it was being spent, and whether he would outlive it. He did not want to be supported by his children. On this point, he and Mom had been equally adamant. Although Dad was concerned about his finances, sometimes poring over his latest bank statement, he wasn't interested in being proactive and letting me help him with budgeting and calculating just how far his money would go. And so I just let him talk.

Soon after I arrived, to give Dad space, I busied myself in Mom's garden. Besides, I couldn't leave the garden Mom loved so well unattended. After I tamed and tidied it, I filled her pots with plants from the garden. I dug iris bulbs and perennial geraniums out of the garden and planted them in her pots. I scoured Mom's and Tracy's gardens for any other perennials that might work well in the pots. I arranged them together on the little veranda and propped the white cross inlaid with bits of mirror, which Mom had elsewhere in her garden, in one of the pots. I cut some flowers, especially Mom's much-loved strelitzias and, with Dad's permission, put them in a vase on the dining room table. With all that under control, I watered the garden.

As I watered, Dad came out, drink in hand, and sat in his usual chair on the veranda next to the back door.

"Your Mom would be so proud of you!"

I stopped watering, poured myself a glass of wine, and joined Dad on the veranda. We chatted; we spoke about whatever Dad wanted to talk about. And he wanted to talk about Mom.

"I'll be honest with you," Dad said to me. "I miss your mother."

I nodded. His grief and loss were written all over him.

"What do you miss about Mom?" I asked.

I thought he might say her cooking or how well she took care of him and all the things she did for him.

"Her personality," he replied. "I miss her personality."

I was touched by his openness but didn't delve any deeper, and Dad didn't take the conversation any further.

With the garden somewhat tidier, Dad became a little more engaged in it too. He asked me to trim the parts of the tree and creeper that tickled his head when he walked underneath them. He searched his workshop for a saw so I could cut back the hedge and trees that were growing over from the neighbor's yard and canopying the walkway. He called my nephew, Jared, to come and help me with the branches I couldn't reach.

That afternoon, while we sat on the veranda and surveyed our work, Johanna swept the long pathway.

"I've always wanted to do this, but the old man says, 'No, leave the outside, just clean the inside,'" she told me afterwards.

Dad was a take-me-as-you-find-me kind of guy. He wasn't one for putting on his best face to impress others. He appreciated plain speaking and certainly instilled that in me. While I was visiting with Dad, I reconnected with members of our extended family, including having coffee with one of my aunts. When she dropped me off, she came in to say hello.

As we approached the door to the cottage, my aunt blurted out, "Oh no, look at your Mom's poor garden. It was her pride and joy."

"I've already worked in it," I replied. "You should have seen it before."

Dad sat in his spot on the couch watching TV.

"Hello, Ken."

Dad greeted my aunt in return. They visited while I made us a cup of tea.

Afterwards, I saw my aunt out to her car. "Brenda," she said, "Your dad sure keeps his place clean. It's spotless."

I agreed with her, saw her off, and went back inside.

Dad was now on his kitchen stool having a drink. I started to wash the teacups and told him about my visit with my aunt. As I dried one of the cups, I came and stood near Dad as we chatted. I mentioned to him my aunt's compliment about his home being so well-kept and spotless. Dad looked pleased. And then I added, "Unlike you."

At first Dad seemed taken aback at the frankness of my comment. He hesitated for a moment and then he burst out laughing, "That's what I like," he said. "Say it as it is."

CHAPTER SIXTEEN

"Miss Ann!"

Dad had come across to the main house to find me.

"I'm in the living room." I set my book down on the coffee table and got up from the couch.

"Can you help me?" Dad passed me his outdated cell phone. "Alan sent me a message about the car. But I must tell him that Clinton is dealing with it and he doesn't need to get that part for me. Can you reply to him?"

I started to spell out the message to Dad's mechanic, pressing each key the required number of times to arrive at the letter I needed.

"My fingers are too big for that little phone," Dad said.

I focused on my typing as he asked, "Miss Ann, won't you cut my nails for me?"

I glanced up and followed his gaze to a nail clipper lying on the coffee table. The message finished and sent on its way, I reached for the clipper, held Dad's hand, and started to trim his nails.

"The one I have is old and doesn't cut well, so I couldn't do it myself."

I trimmed too closely. Dad flinched.

"Sorry."

I adjusted how short I trimmed the nails and finished both hands.

"Thank you," Dad said. He got up and hobbled his way back to the cottage.

Most of the conversations between Dad and me happened in short bursts. He would think of something and pass a comment or ask a question, and I would reply. A couple more exchanges might follow, after which I would leave the conversation alone.

I knew that one of Dad's irritations with me was that, according to him, I asked too many questions. I couldn't just know something, I needed to know the details, the context, and the personal responses to what had happened.

Dad, on the other hand, was not curious about those things. So something happened, so what? His sentiment was that if it had no impact on him, then it wasn't for him to try to change it, and it certainly wasn't any of his business. "Live and let live" was his mantra.

During my visit, I decided to follow Dad's thought process instead of my own, hence the short bursts of flow in our conversations, like the one we had one day when he asked me, "What day did your mother die?"

The question came out of nowhere and I found it strange that he seemed to not know.

"June 23," I replied, closing the door of the refrigerator after retrieving the jug of milk.

"It is almost two years ago."

"Yes, and it still feels like yesterday."

"Yes, it does," Dad responded.

I decided not to dig any deeper into his feelings, and left the conversation there.

On another occasion, again out of nowhere, Dad said, "You can't make people change. You have to accept them as they are, as well as the things that they do. People will do what they do."

I chose not to ask what in particular he might be referring to. I merely replied, "Yes, I know. I've given up trying to change anyone."

Towards the end of my stay, I noticed a subtle change in Dad. The weekend before I left, Clinton was installing a new window in the kitchen of the main house. Dad sat in his usual morning spot, watching Clinton work. As I dried a plate, I came to stand next to him. I too looked across the courtyard to see what my brother was doing.

"Good job, Clinton," Dad said, out of my brother's hearing. As though he'd just realized that, he followed it with, "I should go and compliment my son."

"That's a good idea," I replied. "Compliments are always welcome."

Dad hobbled over to the other side on one crutch to praise my brother for a job well done.

Since the beginning of my visit, I'd had an evening routine of heading for bed by 8:30 or 9:00 every night. I didn't find my time with Dad during the day taxing, but my reserves were low nonetheless. After dinner with the family, I usually spent the rest of the evening reading in my room. Going to bed early meant that I awoke early in the morning too.

In the mornings I would patter down the hallway into the kitchen and put on the kettle. Before long, one or all four of the dogs would come to greet me. My favorite was Benjamin, a black Labrador-cross. As a young dog he had been full-bodied and powerful, but now he was older, slower, and graying, yet he still exuded a warm and selfless demeanor. When he was lucky enough to be the first to come and greet me, I would sneak him a treat. But we needed to be quick, because it wouldn't be long before the kitchen filled with four-legged bodies.

Once my tea had steeped and I'd added milk, I'd pad back to my bedroom with my cup of tea and a rusk. After shutting the door on four expectant faces, I would pull back the curtains to let the morning light stream in. My moment of pleasure came when I climbed back into bed and dipped my rusk, a hard, twice-baked biscuit, in my tea to soften it before eating it. As I dipped and ate my rusk and drank the tea, I would look out at the garden. The dogs often wandered past the window and sniffed around in the flower beds. A cat might stalk a pigeon sitting on the grass. Cape sparrows flitted about in the autumn air and the doves always cooed and cooed.

Once I had finished my tea, I would reach for the devotional *Jesus Calling* and my Bible. It was my time with the Lord.

April 19, 2016 was one such morning. I was in my room enjoying my quiet time, sitting in bed with my cup of tea, curtains pulled back, the morning glow on the garden. I had read the devotional reading for that day and it had felt, to me, like just words on the page. My visit with my father was coming to an end and I was concerned for him. I was sure God had more for me that morning. So I turned the pages and stopped on the reading for August 23. The direction from God was clear and vibrant.

Based on the reading, I wrote what I believed God was saying to me in my journal:

Entrust your loved ones to me; release them into my protective care. They are much safer with me than in your clinging hands. If you let a loved one become an idol in your heart, you endanger that one—as well as yourself. When you release your loved one to me, you are free to cling to my hand. As you entrust others into my care, I am free to shower blessings on them. My presence will go with them wherever they go, and I will give them rest. The same Presence stays with you, as you relax and place your trust in Me. Watch to see what I will do.

I sensed that God was again telling me to not worry about my family and, in particular, my father. To pray for him and to love him, but not to worry about him. In fact, I felt that he was telling me to leave Dad alone and entrust him to God. The more I worried about my father, the more he became an idol in my life, and the more I stood in the way of God working in his life and blessing him. God had a plan and I needed to step aside in faith. Those were encouraging words for me as I only had two days left to spend with Dad; my flight was leaving later the following evening. I also sensed God telling me that I was not Dad's rescuer. I was not responsible for his choices. He was not a reflection on me. Instead, I am a reflection of my Father in heaven.

One of the Bible verses for the devotional was Ephesians 3:20, "*Now to him who is able to do immeasurably more than all we ask or imagine, according to his power that is at work within us,*" part of Paul's prayer for the church at Ephesus. I read the entire prayer and then, getting down on my knees, I prayed it in paraphrase through for my father, entrusting him to God's care. This is what I prayed:

In Christ and through faith in him I may approach God with freedom and confidence. For this reason I kneel before the Father, from whom every family in heaven and on earth derives its name. I pray that out of his glorious riches he may strengthen Dad with power through his Spirit in Dad's inner being, so that Christ may dwell in Dad's heart through faith. And I pray that Dad, being rooted and established in love, may have power, together with all the saints, to grasp how wide and long and high and deep is the love of Christ, and to know this love that surpasses knowledge—that Dad may be filled to the measure of all the fullness of God. Now to him who is able to do immeasurably more than all I ask or imagine, according to his power that is at work within me, to him be glory in the church and in Christ Jesus throughout all generations, for ever and ever! Amen (Ephesians 3:12, 14-21).

The next day, my last morning, I knelt and prayed those verses again. I entrusted my father wholly to God's care as I had been told to do. Around 9:00 I went over to Dad's cottage to have my breakfast. He was in his usual spot in the kitchen when I walked in.

"Morning, Dad."

"Morning, Miss Ann."

I looked at him and stopped. "Are you okay?"

I had made a point of not commenting on Dad's appearance, but on this day he looked decidedly unwell. His face was swollen and flushed. Mucous ran from his nose. His eyes were weeping.

"It's just hay fever," he said.

It's autumn, not spring. But I decided not to press the matter.

Dad had been adamant that he was not going to see any doctors. He wasn't interested in another stint in the hospital. He didn't want to go anywhere for any reason. He wanted to be at home. He had softened in many ways, but he was still extremely stubborn about his health. Later that morning, the swelling of his face had subsided, and his eyes and nose were no longer excreting fluids.

"You look so much better than this morning," I said to him as he sat on the couch.

"It's hay fever," he said again.

"Well, it certainly causes your face to swell," I replied.

"Yes, and my nose runs."

And we left the discussion there.

That evening, Dad had his bath while I watched TV. He managed to get in and out by himself before hobbling across the living room to his bedroom. "Good night, Miss Ann. See you in the morning."

He couldn't have forgotten that I was leaving within the hour for the airport. We had spoken about it before he took his bath.

"No, you won't," I replied.

"Oh yes, I forgot," he said.

I got up and in the doorway of his bedroom we exchanged a kiss.

"Goodbye. I enjoyed our visit," I said to Dad, diverting my eyes and moving back into the living room.

"I enjoyed it too," he said with warmth in his voice as he was enveloped by the darkness of his bedroom.

I finished tidying Dad's cottage, putting it back the way he liked it before switching off the TV. I walked to the doorway of his bedroom and, into the darkness, said, "Bye".

There was the slightest pause then Dad replied, "Bye". He matched my tone and pitch exactly.

Lord, is he crying? I asked in my heart. Was the pause so that he could swallow his tears and get his voice under control? The exact tone and pitch, was that another cover-up?

I turned from the door and took those thoughts and questions with me. I left Dad in the privacy of his darkened bedroom. God had already told me to back off and leave my father and my family in his care. I locked up and went across to the main house to do some last-minute things before heading off to the airport and the long trip home to Canada.

Just five days later, on the morning of April 26, Clinton and Tracy found Dad dead in the bathtub. He'd taken his last bath sometime the night before and, while in the tub, suffered a cerebral hemorrhage. His suffering was over.

CHAPTER SEVENTEEN

Michiel and I returned to South Africa for Dad's funeral. My brother, Grant, was coming from Australia and it might be one of the last times the siblings would be together. It was important to me to be with the family to say goodbye to Dad.

As with Mom, I wanted to prepare a eulogy for Dad, but I really didn't know what I was going to say. Mom's eulogy had been easy to prepare. We had a close bond and an affinity for each other. Dad and I didn't have that. Mom was a model person in many ways; her faults were not glaringly obvious. She was well liked and much loved. There was a rich history to draw on. Dad, on the other hand, was the opposite.

We had little in common. He could be difficult to draw close to and there were many layers of hurt and misunderstanding in our relationship. What did I say about a person I found to be distant and cantankerous? A person who was adept at isolating himself and hurting those close to him, and whose best friend was a quart of beer?

How could I give a eulogy that was honest yet kind—one that portrayed Dad as he was? A eulogy that rang true and also did not dishonor him?

I sat at the same table where Dad and I just weeks before had eaten breakfast and I started to write and tell our story. I wasn't quite sure where it was going to go or how it was going to turn out. I prayed, as I often do before I write, and I started to type.

It took me more than six hours to write and edit a eulogy that I would read in twelve minutes. And in that process God revealed Dad's contribution to my life, a contribution that I had mostly ignored. For most of my life, my focus had been on what our relationship was not, with little regard to contemplating and appreciating what Dad had been able to give me.

Dad would never have described himself as a feminist, and nor would I, or anyone who knew him, have. But he was. In the early 1970s, when I was a girl of about six or seven, I overheard Dad speaking with one of my aunts about the purpose of investing in further education for girls. My aunt commented that she would not pay for a daughter to go to university. In fact, it would be a waste of money as daughters would just get married, have children, and stay at home. That argument did not hold water with my father. He was firmly in the opposite camp, believing that girls should have access to higher education, and that they should be encouraged to go. I clearly remember his response to my aunt's comments, "Well, my daughter will have the opportunity to go to university."

Dad held education in high regard as he believed that it was the key to getting ahead in life. He wanted that for all his children. There was no double standard between girls and boys in Dad's mind. His daughter would have access to all the opportunities that he would afford his sons. That may be regarded as the norm today in the western world, but that wasn't the case back in the sixties and seventies. I grew up with Dad's mantra that I was to go to university drummed into me. It was a given; I didn't argue with it.

Dad valued education because it was something he didn't have. He trained as an electrician, and later became a salesman selling batteries to the goldmines. He would often say, "There's a lot that can be taken from you, but once you have it, no one can ever take away your education." It's no wonder that after Mom died two of the few books Dad still wanted to keep in the cottage were dictionaries.

It was only in my forties that I realized the university education I had always taken for granted was actually a gift. Many women before me had fought for the right to vote, the right to obtain a higher education, and the right to pursue a career of their choice. I grew up in an era where a lot of that had happened or was in the process of unfolding. Dad opened that door for me. By giving me the gift of education, he equipped me with choices in life.

It was also a gift to me because I love to learn. I love to gain knowledge. I first realized that when I went back to university, at the age of twenty-six, to get my post-graduate Diploma in Education at the University of the Witwatersrand in Johannesburg. I wanted to teach.

As we drove home after class one day, I excitedly recounted to Dan, my first husband, what I had learned in my 'Pursuit of History' class that day. As we hurtled down the highway, heading south from Johannesburg towards our home, he turned to me and said, "You love to learn. You will always study."

Years later, when my husband Michiel and I were talking about how much I like to learn and gain knowledge, I chuckled and said, "I don't know where I get it from."

Michiel replied, "Your father, you get it from your father. He is an intelligent man."

I had never, not once, thought of my father as intelligent. I hadn't noticed that attribute in him. I was too busy noticing his faults. His love of and capacity for education and learning existed, it had just never been fulfilled in his life, and it took an outsider to notice.

In preparing the eulogy, I also realized that Dad had raised me to be a straight speaker. Sometimes I wish that he hadn't, but he had. Dad was a guy who said it like it was and he appreciated others who spoke plainly.

When I was about seven years old, I developed a stutter. I remember coming out of the back door of our house in Carey Street one day to say something to Dad. I started to speak, but I stuttered and stammered the words. Dad interrupted me and said, "Stop. Think about what you want to say then say it, and say it only once." He wasn't one for the soft touch. I moved past my stutter phase pretty quickly after that.

I took Dad's advice to heart and, like him, I became a straight speaker. In my circle of friends, I am known as the one who will give you honest, uncluttered feedback. I hope, though, that I have learned to temper my straight talk with Mom's softer touch.

A friend once described me as the person she comes to when she needs a reality check in her life. Another commented that she always knows where she stands with me, and she likes that. A close friend has said that, when she asks me for feedback, she has learned that she needs to be prepared to hear the answer. She has come to appreciate that I don't take sides, but I see and express the other party's perspective too. I take those comments as compliments and a testimony to Dad's influence in my life.

Dad was not someone to run other people down or say negative things about them. Even as an adult, if I commented negatively about someone Dad would call me on it. On a visit to South Africa, I was espousing my opinion on the breaking news of athlete Oscar Pistorius's arrest for the death of his girlfriend Reeva Steenkamp. Dad stopped me and asked, "Were you there? Did you see it happen? You don't know what happened."

He was right. I needed to be more cautious about jumping to conclusions and spouting forth opinions. Dad didn't jump to conclusions; he didn't find it necessary to comment on other people's lives and choices.

In writing the eulogy, I realized too that Dad had showed his love for me in the ways he knew how. From the time I was a teen, and even when I was a young adult, he'd say to me, "If you are ever in trouble, call me and I will come and get you. It doesn't matter where you are in the world, I will come and get you."

And there were times when I would have a fight with Dan before we married and I did call my parents to come and get me. Dad would drive to Jo'burg with Mom, pack my things into the car, and take me home. In due course, I would return to my boyfriend and somewhere in the future there would be a rinse and repeat cycle. I never heard a grumble from Dad or Mom. Perhaps I should have, but I didn't.

Another way Dad showed his love for me was to paint my first bachelor flat on De Korte Street in Johannesburg, and later the cottage I stayed in after I was widowed. Dad painted the bachelor flat a warm yellow and the cottage a refreshing cream. When Dad was painting the cottage, he spent two weekends with me on my property south of

Johannesburg. I had rented out the main house and moved into the cottage. Dad said he would give it a fresh lick of paint. On the Saturday morning, he and Mom would come through, we'd have a cup of tea together, and Mom and I would visit while Dad painted. After Mom left, Dad would paint the rest of the day, sleep over on the Saturday night, and paint again on Sunday morning before Mom came to get him and take him home. Dad did not drink on either of the weekends and we had a congenial time together.

Later, when Mom went down to Durban to run the Comrades Marathon, I drove to Springs to visit with Dad while he was on his own. We had a good visit and he prepared a barbeque for us.

When I started to date Michiel, Dad asked me about him. I remember sitting on the arm of Dad's chair in the living room, my arm strung across the back of the chair, telling him about this new man in my life. And it was Dad who later said to me, "You are going to marry him." When I asked how he knew, he replied, "Because your face lights up whenever you talk about him."

Dad came to be fond of Michiel and would often refer to him as 'Champion'. Dad could see that Michiel took good care of me and that we were happy together. I think that pleased him.

'Miss Ann' was Dad's term of endearment for me. When I was little, Mom called me 'Brookies' and my Grandmother James called me 'Sally'. I outgrew both those names, but I never outgrew 'Miss Ann' with Dad. I liked the name and, in my twenties, I named my Staffordshire bull terrier, Miss Ann.

Many influences have made me the woman I am today: my mother, my husbands, my relationship with the Lord, my faith in God, the prompting of the Holy Spirit, my own emotional make-up, my desires and my sinfulness, my friends, my mistakes and my accomplishments, my hometown, my brothers and, of course, my father.

I have come to realize that my father played a greater role in fashioning me into the woman I am than I ever gave him credit for. The negative aspects of our relationship have fashioned me, and so have the positive ones.

CHAPTER EIGHTEEN

More than any event in my life, Mom's death has been the most profound for me. I have never known such intense emotional pain. I know that God was with me during that time. Together with the psalmist I can say, *"Whom have I in heaven but you? And earth has nothing I desire besides you. My flesh and my heart may fail, but [you are] the strength of my heart and my portion forever"* (Psalm 73:25-26).

When my heart was broken and my spirit grieved, God upheld and guided me. As I trusted God with my broken heart, he guided me to show me the great love he had for my father. And through my father, he has shown me the great love he has for the entire human race.

God's love is a love that loves us right where we are, unconditionally. This love from God was a love I had not given credence to before. And his love is a love that I cannot love on my own. He transformed my heart, opening it to love my earthly father in a new way, his way. God showed me the way forward: the way of courage, the way of healing, the way of transformation, the way of Jesus. I was able to love my Dad compassionately when I stepped away from my need to have him be anyone in my life other than who he was, my lost, broken father. My heart came to ache at his emotional, physical, and spiritual suffering.

Albert Nolan explains how, like the wealthy young ruler, we find it difficult to "sell all our possessions" and follow Jesus, to give ourselves wholeheartedly to him. I needed to let go, not only of my father, but also my mother in order to give more of myself wholeheartedly to Jesus. I had to give over my grief too.

I could have easily stayed caught up in my sorrow and held onto my mother. I wanted to, but I knew that my heart would become cold and barren. My regret at not being there for my mother could have become a cornerstone in my life. And it may very well have, if not for the kindness of God. In his kindness, he placed challenges before me. He wanted me to choose the right path, the right way. He also showed kindness to me with gentle reminders and loving words.

At the beginning of 2016, he gave me these verses from Acts 17:26b-28, paraphrased in my own words, to meditate on:

God has determined the times set for me and the exact places where I should live. God did this so that men would seek him and perhaps reach out for him and find him, though he is not far from any one of us. For in him, I live and move and have my being. And so too, does every one of his creations.

I was exactly where God wanted me to be. It was part of his purpose that my life had played out the way it had. And even the exercising of personal choices that were contrary to his will for me, and for my mother, he was redeeming for his purposes. The regret I felt was mine. There was no regret for God. I was exactly where he wanted me to be and it was all part of his plan so that others would seek him, and reach out for him—perhaps even my father. And when Dad did, he would find him, as God is not far from any of us. My regret about not being more available to and present with my Mom is still a real regret, and yet I am comforted that it is not God's regret for Mom or me. The lessons God was teaching me were hard, but they drew me ever closer to him.

I was also learning to live from that place of not knowing if all my prayers for Dad had even made a difference in his being reconciled to God. Had he gone to the grave still shaking his fist at God? Despite not knowing, I felt peace at his passing. That was in marked contrast to the angst I felt at Mom's passing. In my economy, it should have been the other way around but, as I have discovered, God's economy can appear amazingly unfair and it is, indeed, perplexingly mysterious. The peace I felt was a gift from God.

In his infiniteness kindness, God gave me the opportunity to finish well with my father, to say goodbye, to show him love, kindness, and acceptance, and to have closure in our relationship in this life. It wasn't God's will for me to have the same opportunity with my mother. Instead there was to be a severe wounding and scarring that God will use for his purpose, if I let him.

On May 27, 2016, a month after Dad's death, I wrote in my journal:

Lord, you have given me the gift of peace. Not knowing Dad's final destination, I could be wracked with sadness and serious thoughts and yet you have given me peace. I did what you sent me to do. I went to spend time with Dad. I accepted him as he was. I listened when you told me to let go and entrust him to you. I believed you when you said that you would take care of him. And so I trust that—whatever the outcome.

A week later, June 2, 2016, I wrote this:

Lord, was Dad crying when I went to say goodbye to him? Did his heart turn at that moment? Shirley (my cousin) mentioned how proud he looked when he told her that his daughter had come to visit him. As I read in Max Lucado's *The Power of a Simple Prayer*, if all we can summon is a plaintive "Oh Father" that is enough. The faith of a mustard seed, tears on a pillow, the softening of a heart, the slightest chink in his armor. Unconditional love—the love of the Father. You showed me how to love like you love. *"There is but one God, the Father, from whom all things come and for whom I live; and there is but one Lord, Jesus Christ, from whom all things come and through whom I live"* (1 Corinthians 8:6).

I did not know the outcome of my father's eternal destiny, and it was a concern for me. Yet whenever my thoughts became anxious about

Dad and where he stood with God at the time of his death, God's peace would fill me.

Dad always gave the distinct impression that he had no interest in God whatsoever. He liked to say that he was a Baptist, a bush-Baptist. That was his way of deriding Christian beliefs and denominations and aligning himself with not having a faith in God. Occasionally he came to Midnight Mass with us at Christmas, but for the most part he didn't darken the door of a church, at least not of his own accord.

After Mom died, Dad asked me to go through and sort her things, including all her books, as Mom was an avid reader.

"I don't want any of the books," Dad said. "Except for the dictionaries and the Bible."

The words slipped easily out of his mouth. Once he realized what he had said, he covered it up and added, "Well, maybe."

I passed Mom's books on to her reading buddy, her sister-in-law, Doreen. I put the two dictionaries and Mom's Bible on the window ledge in Dad's bedroom. I don't know that he ever cracked the Bible open in the next twenty-two months of his life, but his slip of the tongue showed that he was more open to God and the Bible than he even allowed himself to admit.

There were times when Mom and I would discuss Dad and his lack of belief in God. During one of our regular telephone conversations, she recounted how, sometimes, she would get home from church earlier on a Sunday morning than expected, and Dad would be watching a Christian TV program. That aside, Dad appeared to show no interest in spiritual matters and asked no questions.

One Sunday in January 2017, our pastor was speaking on the Prodigal Son, the same passage that we chose for my father's funeral. As our pastor finished his sermon, my thoughts were full of my father. I felt the heaviness of his suffering. I felt the sadness of his lostness, the emptiness of a life lived so far from God. I felt despair at his struggles in this life and how it all ended. I was going down that path of heaviness and deep sadness when suddenly a picture of my parents flashed in my mind, a photo my brother, Grant, had taken of my parents at my mother's birthday dinner probably fifteen years before. I didn't even know it existed until Grant posted it on Facebook in memory of my parents after Dad died. In it, my parents are sitting in a restaurant, at a table covered with a white cloth. They are both wearing white and my father has his arm around Mom. Mom is leaning into Dad and they are laughing. Their faces had exploded with smiles that exuded happiness and joy. The first time I saw that photo I became completely still. Not only because their faces were so full of rapture, but because I didn't know them together like that. At least not experiencing happiness and joy to that extent.

As I sat in church that Sunday, my mind going down a rabbit trail of despair and discouragement, that was the photo that flashed in my mind, and I heard the words, "Brenda, this is who your parents are now."

I believe that God was telling me that my parents are together and that they are filled with indescribable joy in his presence. They are now all that he ever intended them to be. Their relationship is pure and complete in him. I was comforted and I am grateful for God's kindness in revealing this to me. What a glorious outcome!

As I pondered this, my thoughts led me to ask: does all the suffering that came before still matter? No doubt, my parents' suffering was now over. Should I hold onto the image of that picture, and the knowledge of their eternal happiness, and let all that went before go? Does it no longer matter?

I have to conclude that it does matter. Mom's experience matters, particularly for those who follow after her and who, like Mom, don't have private medical insurance and rely on the services of the public healthcare system in South Africa. I have to conclude that God did not allow the deep wounding of my heart, the deep wounding of my brothers' hearts, or that of my nephews and sister-in-law, for no particular reason. That wounding matters. It matters because my mother's life had value.

Dad's lostness and rebellion matter. They matter because hurt people hurt people. A cycle of hurt has tendrils that reach far and wide and affect many, particularly those closest to the hurt individual. It matters because any addiction is a means of coping and escape, and often prevents the addict from maturing emotionally and coming to a place of repentance, forgiveness, and healing. Yet, even in his lostness and in the final stages of alcoholism, my father and his life had value, as hard as it might have been for most people to see.

Every life has value, and God cares how we live in this life. The purpose of our life on earth isn't merely to attain eternal glory. Rather, for me, it is about heaven coming down to earth; it is about God's name being hallowed. It is about his kingdom coming on earth. It is about his will being done in my life, and in your life, and in the lives of others, as it is in heaven. It's about living with purpose in this life, in submission and obedience to him. It's about caring for the lost, the poor, and the broken. It's about being his hands and feet in this world.

God took me deeper into that place of submission and obedience to him as I watched my mother die. He transformed me into a more trusting follower of Jesus in the months that followed. He taught me to love my father with his love and, in so doing, he put his love for the human race in my heart.

"*For God so loved the world*"—you, me, the drunk, the atheist, the perpetrator of crime, the fascist, the environmentalist, the grandmother, the unborn child—"*that he sent his one and only Son, that whoever believes in him shall not perish but have eternal life*" (John 3:16).

I am the conduit of God's love in this world. I am his temple, his hands, his feet, the evidence of his compassion and his all-embracing love. I am his follower, his foot-soldier, his daughter, and his friend. I am here to do the will of the Father, fulfilling his mission for my life. He takes all my pain and heartache and transforms them into something beautiful for his purpose. He does that for all who know him and love him, for all who obey him and trust him. He is the God of restoration. He is the God of redemption and the sower of dreams.

While my mother was still alive, I sat at her bedside one day, contemplating the bare walls of her hospital room. I took in their depressing, impersonal, bland neutrality. Not even the walls cared. It shouldn't be like this. The walls should exude warmth. Even in death there should be hope and warmth. Not this cold, stark indifference. As I sat there, God seeded a dream in my heart.

When I flicked the cockroach off my mother's sheet, preventing it from crawling onto her, the dream took root. The roots sank deeper with each bit of evidence of the apathy of the nursing staff. This was not what nursing should look like. This was not how the sick and dying should be cared for. This was so far from the center of care.

God stirred in me the dream of a hospital in my mother's memory, one where care and compassion would be paramount, just as they had been in my mother's life. A place where the doctors and the nurses saw the patients as individuals loved by God, and extended love and respect to them in their dark and difficult times. A place of real hope, with warm, vibrant colors on the walls. God gave me a dream of funds no longer being siphoned off from the hospital, but once again being directed to the care of the poor and those who could not afford the exorbitant costs of private medical treatment.

At first I dreamed of a new hospital on the outskirts of Springs, perhaps on the road between Dunnottar and Nigel, a road I had traveled numerous times with Mom. It seemed fitting, as Mom had lived almost all of her life in Springs and her last years in Sharon Park, Nigel. But God directed my gaze from the dusty tracts of land between Dunnottar and Nigel, to the beast itself, Charlotte Maxeke Johannesburg Academic Hospital.

God redeems. It is what he does and who he is. He redeems a broken world through Jesus. He transforms and makes all things new through his Holy Spirit. And so, of course, he would want to redeem the hospital itself. My gaze moved from those open pieces of land filled with African dust, baked by the African sun, to the drab hallways of the hospital. It took me past the impersonal nurses' desk, past the general ward, to my mother's airless, windowless death chamber. It was there in that room, on that floor, in that cancer ward, that God wanted to start redeeming its brokenness.

My dream is for warmth on the walls, equipment that works, medication that is freely given, and compassionate care for the sick and dying. I dream that the nurses are valued for what they do, that they are remunerated well for their services, and that they are themselves taken care of so that they can extend care to their patients. I dream of a hospital that is a place of refuge and safety. A place where the sick can become well and the dying are loved and valued. A place where they can die with respect and dignity because the nurses are caring, diligent in their work, and trained in palliative care.

I dream of a hospital where the doctors are less concerned about their reputations, their future careers as private practitioners, and the money and status with which they will be rewarded, and more concerned about loving care for all, upholding the Hippocratic Oath. A hospital should never be a place where patients are shouted at, have their gauze and bandages ripped off their faces, or are looked at and treated as scurvy strays in the street no one wants to touch. They should not be left carelessly to die. Medical professionals have lost their souls when they let that happen on their watch.

I have a dream that doctors "will remember that there is art to medicine as well as science ... warmth, sympathy, and understanding." I dream that they "will remember that they do not treat a fever chart, a cancerous growth, but a sick human being, whose illness may affect the person's family and economic stability. Their responsibility includes these related problems, if they are to care adequately for the sick" (excerpts from the Hippocratic Oath).

I have a dream of a hospital that does the name of Charlotte Maxeke, a woman of faith, a woman of social justice, proud. And a hospital where hope is extended. A real hope, not a false hope. A hope that is in keeping with the reality of the situation so that the family is informed and can make the right decisions for their loved one. A hope that allows the family and the person who is ill to prepare well for the end of this life and the transition to the next.

I carry this dream in my heart and in my prayers, knowing that my God has counseled me: "Brenda, keep your thoughts focused on me. Keep your prayers—day and night, night and day—filling my heavens. I hear them and, in due course, at the appointed time, I move to fulfill my will."

I know too that "*the only thing that counts is faith expressing itself through love*" (Galatians 5:6b), and that my mother's death did not go unnoticed by God because "*precious in the sight of the Lord is the death of his saints*" (Psalm 116:15).

And so I dream, and I pray. I trust, and I hope. And I wait. I wait for the Holy Spirit to move and fulfill the will of God. And as I wait, I meditate on these words, based on Psalm 62:7-9 and 11-12:

My salvation and my honor depend on God,
he is my mighty rock, my refuge.
I trust in him at all times;
I pour out my heart to him,
for God is my refuge.
Lowborn men and women are but a breath,
the highborn are but a lie;
if weighed on a balance, they are nothing;
together they are only a breath.
One thing God has spoken,
two things have I heard:
that you, O God, are strong,
and that you, O Lord, are loving.
Surely you will reward each person
according to what he has done.

Mom and Dad at Mom's birthday dinner,
October 2001 in Springs, South Africa.

Mom and Dad with my brother, Mark, circa 1964 on Durban beach, KwaZulu-Natal, South Africa.

The first photo of Mom and me, 1967 in the backyard of my grandparents' home in Springs, South Africa.

*Mom and me, with my brother, Mark, on a beach holiday,
circa 1969 KwaZulu-Natal, South Africa.*

*Dad and Mom on Table Mountain, December 1973,
in Cape Town, South Africa.*

Mom, me and the quince tree, circa 1992 in the garden of my home in Johannesburg, South Africa.

Our favourite photo, circa 1993 at the poolside of my home in Johannesburg, South Africa.

The only photo I have of the three of us taken when Dad and Mom visited us in Vancouver, Canada in 1998.

Mom fooling around wearing a wicker basket on her bald head as a hat, March 2010, while on holiday together in KwaZulu-Natal, South Africa.

AFTERWORD

In writing this book, my sister Brenda reveals her instinctive vocation as a bridge-builder, willing to move across the boundaries that mark one church from another. Brenda is at heart ecumenical. Unlike me, who has always remained faithful to the tradition of our upbringing in the Catholic faith, in her writing, Brenda constantly moves beyond denominational boundaries to embrace the wisdom that can be found in various traditions, be they Evangelical or Catholic, the charismatic or the mystical.

We need more of this spirit in our churches, in our communities, in our countries and across the globe. Instead of building walls to keep people out, we need to step out of our boats and walk on the chaotic waters—to move beyond the boundaries we establish between ourselves and others—and take the risk of listening to, hearing, and being receptive to the voices of the others in our world, those who are different from us and who therefore may seem to threaten us.

Brenda and I grew up in apartheid South Africa where, from young, we were schooled in the art of despising those who were different from us and loving those who were the same as us. We learnt to fear, reject, possibly hate, and certainly exclude those who were different. In this book, Brenda shows us that this is not the Christian way. It is not the Christian way to live in safe ghettos with those who are similar to us. Rather, we are challenged by Jesus to reach out in love and compassion to others, especially those who are suffering and marginalized in church and society.

Jesus' compassionate ministry and his proclamation of God's coming reign sought to overcome these distinctions between peoples. He initiated bridge-building as the Christian task in the world, a world where we prefer to stay at home, in what we know and find comforting, rather than face our fears and the unknown that unsettles us. The death of a loved one is the most disruptive and unsettling moment of life, yet, as Brenda attempts to show, when faced in Christ it can lead us to a new life of greater compassion for others who suffer and face death. Growing in acceptance of a loved one's death is also a preparation for accepting the inevitability of our own death in faith and trust.

Brenda challenges us all to move beyond the boundaries of what is consoling and comfortable, to face the challenge of life and to become bridge-builders to others, especially the suffering and the marginalized. Brenda reminds us that we are all called to anticipate this new world of grace, mercy, love and compassion that Jesus announced as the coming reign of God by living courageously in the face of adversity.

Mark James OP
Springs, South Africa
March 26, 2018

FINAL WORDS

Our lives are filled with challenges and heartaches.

Sometimes we are able to find a way through our difficulties and tragedies, thereby experiencing some measure of recovery and healing. Other times we find coping mechanisms that serve us, at least for a while. Then there are times that we get stuck. We are impacted by the tragedy to such an extent that it now defines who we are. We are what happened to us. Forgiveness and healing are far from us, and we don't know how to move forward, or if we even want to.

Grief is no different. I am still tempted to stay in my grief. Grief, though, is not something we leave behind, but something we learn to live with. That shift in perspective helped me to continue on the personal inner journey that is grief. The good news is that it isn't a journey we have to walk alone.

We can implement good practices in our daily living, as well as find groups and resources that help us make sense of our loss, our trauma, and our heartache.

A friend's son died unexpectedly in his early thirties and she describes the pain of his death equal to that of being kicked in the chest by a horse. Sometimes we may feel that the pain of our loss could kill us and that we will never survive it.

I found that my times of morning quiet were a crucial part of my grieving process. Most times I read my Bible and journaled. But there were times all I could do was sit in the dark, and just be.

Reading my Bible was an integral part of processing my grief and communicating with God. His Word is a balm. It heals and gives life. We ignore it at our peril. Journaling was a healing way for me to respond to God's Word and to explore my emotions and questions. It became a concrete way to process my grief and express my loss.

During this time, I found it necessary to pull away from aspects of my social life and from some friendships—for a period of time. I didn't have the emotional capacity for frivolity and light-heartedness. It seemed so empty to me and only accentuated my deep grief and loss. I maintained social engagements with close couple-friends because that provided me with the support of my husband as well as friends who would give me space, support, or listening ears as needed.

I also maintained my weekly walk with a long-time friend. Exercise is an important part of physical, emotional, and psychological health. But more than that, my regular walk gave me the opportunity to talk with a trusted friend who would listen. Once I had spoken enough about my grief I said to her, "I can't talk about this anymore. Not because it doesn't hurt, but because I just need to stop talking about it." And so we did. However, on occasion, whenever I needed to, I would still revisit my grief with her.

I didn't stop going to church, but for a number of months I needed to leave as soon as the service was over. I could not participate in the after-service chit-chat. Nor did I have any capacity to respond to the genuine expressions of concern and explain how I was doing. Gradually, I was able to stay after the service and participate in the socializing.

However, many months and even a year after my mother's death, there were times I would become emotionally upset after church. I would apologize to whomever I was speaking with and say, "I'm sorry, I am not doing well. I need to leave."

Part of healing is recognizing what our needs are, expressing them, and taking care of ourselves. Counseling and participating in recovery groups are beneficial ways to do just that. They help us to identify our emotional needs, to find ways to express them, and, in doing so, to be able to take better care of ourselves.

I found that GriefShare helped me, as it provided me with one evening each week to express and feel my grief. The rest of the week I needed to put my grief on the back burner so as to focus on my work. Even though at times I dragged myself through my day, putting one foot in front of the other, it wasn't something I felt I could fully display at my work place. However, on Monday nights at GriefShare I could let it all out, release the tears, and feel the pain.

GriefShare gave me a structure not only to experience my grief, but to understand its process. I learned that, when experiencing intense grief, it is quite normal to wish, at times, that you too could die. Thoughts of death when grieving are normal; thoughts of suicide are not. I learned too that no two people grieve the same way, even if we are grieving the same person and had a similar relationship to that person, for example, a child to a parent or a parent to a child. GriefShare offered me tools, guidance, and Biblical truths to help me find my way through the dark maze that is grief. Consider GriefShare if you are going through grief or have unresolved grief from the death of a loved one.

If you have another hurt, habit, or hang-up in your life that isn't related to grief, consider Celebrate Recovery. Celebrate Recovery helped me to understand co-dependency and enabling. There were obvious ways co-dependency and enabling were evident in my life, particularly in relation to my father. However, as I have become more sensitive to them, I have been able to identify other less obvious ways co-dependency and enabling impact my life and my relationships. You do not have to have an addiction to attend Celebrate Recovery. A deep emotional hurt is where addiction starts, and an addiction is a symptom of that deeper hurt. Celebrate Recovery helps to explore and address that deeper hurt, hurt we all have.

Since writing my book, I have participated in the Journey Discipleship Course, again through my church. Journey incorporates prayer, discipleship, and spiritual care to help individuals in their relationships, their sexuality, and their identity. At first I didn't think I needed this program but, through participating in it, I came to understand why my mother's death hit me so hard. I came to understand what the loss of my mother took from me aside from her presence and love. The Journey course also revealed patterns of behavior in my life that have caused me to participate in dysfunction in my close relationships. Journey has strengthened my identity in Jesus and my identity as a woman of worth and value. It has helped me to take further responsibility for my actions and to identify ways to attract and build healthier relationships in my life.

Writing my own story has been both hard and healing for me. Writing our stories is a deep and personal way to explore not only our lives, but also our habits, our hurts and grudges, our relationships, and our preferred methods of coping. It is through writing that we can explore and uncover our true feelings.

You don't have to be a writer to explore your life through writing. All that is necessary is a desire to heal, a stirring within that writing is a safe way to explore life, and a tenacity to turn up and see it through.

About halfway through my writing I stopped. I couldn't write on the topic of my grief anymore. I put my writing aside and wondered if I would ever get back to finishing the book. I didn't know that I could.

It was on a visit to South Africa, during a Sunday service at Rosebank Union Church, Johannesburg, that the pastor preached on Nehemiah's return to Jerusalem to rebuild the city's wall. He recounted the challenges and difficulties that Nehemiah and the people of Israel faced. The pastor drew a parallel to our lives and asked what wall had we been building or rebuilding that we had stopped working on. What was it in our lives that we needed to resume building?

I knew that it was my manuscript.

I came home from that trip, picked up my pen, as it were, and continued on the journey of writing my story. The telling of my grief wasn't for anyone else. It was for me and for my own healing. It was a way for me to get the thoughts out of my head and see them on the page. I didn't want to forget what had happened and yet, at the same time, I didn't want the memories to haunt me either. I freed myself from the guilt of forgetting and the torment of remembering by letting the story live on the page rather than in my head.

Perhaps this is you.

Perhaps you would like to explore your story through writing, but don't know where to start or how to persevere when the going gets tough. Or, like me, perhaps you started your story but have put it aside and are unsure if you can or will get back to telling it. Please let me encourage you to return to your manuscript and to continue to unearth and tell your story. It is hard revisiting personal and often painful parts of our lives, but the reward is often a moving forward to live our lives in a new and healthier way.

For just these reasons, I have created an online writing course to assist other women and men to write their stories. My goal is to help you get started writing, to help keep you writing, and to see you accomplish the final telling of your story. You will learn the elements of writing a strong story, get your questions answered, and, most importantly, you will write.

Intrigued? Interested?

Download my eBook, *7 Key Ingredients to Writing a Great Memoir, One that Others will Want to Read,* at **www.brendasmitjames.com** to get a head start.

You don't have to go it alone. We were made for community; we heal better in community. I'd love for you to join us and for us to get to know each other better.

Brenda

Find out more about my online course, workshops, recommended books, and future events on my website at www.brendasmitjames.com.

Here are the websites for the Christian discipleship and recovery courses I recommend:

www.griefshare.org
www.celebraterecovery.ca or www.celebraterecovery.com
www.journeycanada.org

BIBLIOGRAPHY

Eldredge, John. *Waking the Dead: the Glory of a Heart Fully Alive.* Nashville, TN: Thomas Nelson Inc., 2003.

Greig, Pete. *God on Mute: Engaging the Silence of Unanswered Prayer.* Ada, MI: Baker Publishing Group, 2012.

McManus, Erwin Raphael. *The Barbarian Way: Unleash the Untamed Faith Within.* Nashville, TN: Thomas Nelson Inc., 2005.

Nolan, Albert. *Jesus Today: A Spirituality of Radical Freedom.* Cape Town: Double Storey Books, 2006.

Wilkinson, Bruce. *Secrets of the Vine: Breaking Through to Abundance.* Sisters, OR: Multnomah Publishers Inc., 2001.

Van der Vyver, Marita. *Breathing Space.* Middlesex, England: Penguin Books Ltd., 2000.

Young, Sarah. *Jesus Calling: Enjoying Peace in His Presence.* Nashville TN: Thomas Nelson, 2004.

ENDNOTES

[1] Marita Van der Vyver, *Breathing Space* (Middlesex, England: Penguin Books Ltd., 2000), 404-405.

[2] Sarah Young, *Jesus Calling: Enjoying Peace in His Presence* (Nashville TN: Thomas Nelson, 2004), 199.

[3] Sarah Young, *Jesus Calling: Enjoying Peace in His Presence* (Nashville TN: Thomas Nelson, 2004), 146.

[4] Sarah Young, *Jesus Calling: Enjoying Peace in His Presence* (Nashville TN: Thomas Nelson, 2004), 146.

[5] Pete Greig, *God on Mute: Engaging the Silence of Unanswered Prayer* (Ada, MI: Baker Books, 2012), 124-125.

[6] Bruce Wilkinson, *Secrets of the Vine: Breaking Through to Abundance* (Sisters, OR: Multnomah Publishers Inc., 2001), 71.

[7] Bruce Wilkinson, *Secrets of the Vine: Breaking Through to Abundance* (Sisters, OR: Multnomah Publishers Inc., 2001), 72.

[8] Bruce Wilkinson, *Secrets of the Vine: Breaking Through to Abundance* (Sisters, OR: Multnomah Publishers Inc., 2001), 72.

9 Author Unknown, "Introduction: Job" in *The NIV Study Bible, 10th Anniversary Edition: New International Version* (Grand Rapids, MI: Zondervan, 1995), 722-723.

10 Author Unknown, "Introduction: Job" in *The NIV Study Bible, 10th Anniversary Edition: New International Version* (Grand Rapids, MI: Zondervan, 1995), 722-723.

11 Author Unknown, "Introduction: Job" in *The NIV Study Bible, 10th Anniversary Edition: New International Version* (Grand Rapids, MI: Zondervan, 1995), 724.

12 Bruce Wilkinson, *Secrets of the Vine: Breaking Through to Abundance* (Sisters, OR: Multnomah Publishers Inc., 2001), 73-74.

13 Bruce Wilkinson, *Secrets of the Vine: Breaking Through to Abundance* (Sisters, OR: Multnomah Publishers Inc., 2001), 73-74.

14 Bruce Wilkinson, *Secrets of the Vine: Breaking Through to Abundance* (Sisters, OR: Multnomah Publishers Inc., 2001), 73-74.

15 Bruce Wilkinson, *Secrets of the Vine: Breaking Through to Abundance* (Sisters, OR: Multnomah Publishers Inc., 2001), 93.

16 Erwin Raphael McManus, *The Barbarian Way: Unleash the Untamed Faith Within* (Nashville TN: Thomas Nelson, 2005), 23.

17 Erwin Raphael McManus, *The Barbarian Way: Unleash the Untamed Faith Within* (Nashville TN: Thomas Nelson, 2005), 31-32.

18 Erwin Raphael McManus, *The Barbarian Way: Unleash the Untamed Faith Within* (Nashville TN: Thomas Nelson, 2005), 10.

19 Albert Nolan, *Jesus Today: A Spirituality of Radical Freedom* (Cape Town: Double Storey Books, 2006), xvii.

20 Albert Nolan, *Jesus Today: A Spirituality of Radical Freedom* (Cape Town: Double Storey Books, 2006), 83.

[21] Albert Nolan, *Jesus Today: A Spirituality of Radical Freedom* (Cape Town: Double Storey Books, 2006), 85.

[22] Albert Nolan, *Jesus Today: A Spirituality of Radical Freedom* (Cape Town: Double Storey Books, 2006), 67.

[23] John Eldredge, *Waking the Dead* (Nashville TN: Thomas Nelson, 2003), 49.

[24] John Eldredge, *Waking the Dead* (Nashville TN: Thomas Nelson, 2003), 49.

[25] Albert Nolan, *Jesus Today: A Spirituality of Radical Freedom* (Cape Town: Double Storey Books, 2006), 149.

[26] Albert Nolan, *Jesus Today: A Spirituality of Radical Freedom* (Cape Town: Double Storey Books, 2006), 150.

[27] Albert Nolan, *Jesus Today: A Spirituality of Radical Freedom* (Cape Town: Double Storey Books, 2006), 187.

[28] Albert Nolan, *Jesus Today: A Spirituality of Radical Freedom* (Cape Town: Double Storey Books, 2006), 191.